THE ENTREPRENEUR'S SOLUTION

"I agree with Mel's theory: The only way to find out just *how* great we can be is to take an entrepreneurial approach to our future. *The Entrepreneur's Solution* is more than a business mastery blueprint, it's a plan for a successful life."

—**Harvey Mackay**, #1 *New York Times* bestselling author of *Swim With The Sharks*

"Entrepreneurship is the engine that drives our society and creates real change. In this brilliant book, Mel gives you the art of Entrepreneurship from a real world perspective. This is what it takes to build something that is meaningful, successful and sustainable. A must read."

—**Nick Ortner**, *New York Times* bestselling author of *The Tapping Solution*

"Totally fresh air…Mel lifts entrepreneurship above the grind of business operations to the real reason we became entrepreneurs in the first place…to have a life that we loved and one that makes a difference. Practical and transformational all at once."

—**Kevin Ward**, Founder and CEO, YES Master Real Estate

"Entrepreneurs are the agents of change in our world. Through their innovation, resourcefulness, and capabilities, they drive the economic progress of our society. So if you want to really understand the entrepreneurial mind and the courage it requires to be an entrepreneur, check out Mel's new book. In his new book, *The Entrepreneur's Solution*, you'll discover how to define your identity, intentions and ideals as an entrepreneur; the sources of confidence and courage; how to turn adversity into advantage; how to influence and connect with empathy; some of the best ways to collaborate with your customers and other companies; how to make more money while making an impact; and a lot more. Read Mel's book if you want to have game changing growth as an entrepreneur."

—**Joe Polish**, Genius Network

"In today's world of entitlement where people expect a medal just for showing up, Mel Abraham gives us *The Entrepreneur's Solution* to remind us that hard work, and more importantly mind-set, are needed to achieve our goals. If you are ready to start acting, if you are looking for economic freedom, if you are ready to pursue your dreams, Mel's Business Mastery Blueprint will help you transform your business for financial and personal prosperity.

—**Jules Trono**, President and CEO, Compass Business Solutions

"A thought-provoking new way to think about business."

—**Daniel Amen**, MD, author of *Change Your Brain, Change Your Life*

"Mel is the real deal. His teachings will not only show you how to build a successful, profitable, and sustainable business, but also to create your life 'on purpose' so that you have freedom and the lifestyle that you deserve.

This book is a must read, whether you're looking to make the jump from the cubicle to the entrepreneurial world, or if you're already a successful entrepreneur ready to take things to the next level."

—**Mike Wolf**, Serial entrepreneur and Founder of Mike Wolf Mastery

"The *Entrepreneur's Solution* is a must read for you if you are looking for a more holistic approach to building abundance and prosperity.

Mel Abraham lays out a complete blueprint for sustainable success- on how to strengthen the entrepreneur mindset and spirit, sharpen business savvy skills, and financially thrive with passion and commitment. Mel generously shares all of his most influential strategies in creating a business that will allow you to achieve the financial freedom you have always dreamed of, and more importantly allow you to have more choices in your life to serve your family, your community and to contribute to better our planet."

—**Dr. Susanne Bennett**, bestselling author of *The 7-Day Allergy Makeover* and host of the Wellness for Life radio show on RadioMD at iHeart Radio

"Want to learn to shift your mindset, harness your creative force, influence change for a legacy worth leaving to the next generation? If your answer is yes, you need this book. *The Entrepreneur's Solution* is the go to source for creating, expanding and or accelerating a profitable and sustainable business grounded in your authentic values. Mel Abraham has generated a powerhouse book for would be entrepreneurs and serial entrepreneurs seeking ever advancing knowledge of mindset, transformational business and human potential. Make a difference in yourself and your business, read this book!"

—**Suzette Mariel**, author of *Stop Procrastinating! Start Producing!*

THE
ENTREPRENEUR'S
SOLUTION

THE MODERN MILLIONAIRE'S
PATH TO MORE PROFIT, FANS & FREEDOM

MEL H. ABRAHAM

New York

THE ENTREPRENEUR'S SOLUTION
THE MODERN MILLIONAIRE'S PATH TO MORE PROFIT, FANS & FREEDOM

Published in New York, New York, by Morgan James Publishing. Morgan James and The Entrepreneurial Publisher are trademarks of Morgan James, LLC.
www.MorganJamesPublishing.com

The Morgan James Speakers Group can bring authors to your live event. For more information or to book an event visit The Morgan James Speakers Group at
www.TheMorganJamesSpeakersGroup.com.

A **free** eBook edition is available
with the purchase of this print book.

CLEARLY PRINT YOUR NAME ABOVE IN UPPER CASE

Instructions to claim your free eBook edition:
1. Download the BitLit app for Android or iOS
2. Write your name in **UPPER CASE** on the line
3. Use the BitLit app to submit a photo
4. Download your eBook to any device

ISBN 978-1-63047-330-3 paperback
ISBN 978-1-63047-331-0 eBook
Library of Congress Control Number:
2014943483

Interior Design by:
Bonnie Bushman
bonnie@caboodlegraphics.com

In an effort to support local communities and raise awareness and funds, Morgan James Publishing donates a percentage of all book sales for the life of each book to Habitat for Humanity Peninsula and Greater Williamsburg.

Get involved today, visit
www.MorganJamesBuilds.com

Habitat
for Humanity
Peninsula and
Greater Williamsburg
Building Partner

DEDICATION

This book is dedicated to my dad, Joseph Abraham who stood quiet but strong and loved us with everything he had. Dad showed me that, "because it was the right thing to do!" is the way to live life. Thank you for being one of the greatest men in my life!

CONTENTS

The difference between what we do and what we are capable of doing would solve most of the world's problems.
—Mahatma Gandhi

ACKNOWLEDGEMENTS

No success is a solo effort. This is no exception and I have a lot of people that have been an incredible and indelible part of my journey. Some amazing friends, mentors and souls in my life all of which impacted me in someway and live within these pages somehow, have truly blessed me.

To start, my brother from Montana, Brendon Burchard who without his prodding this book would have never happened. I remember us sitting in a boardroom in Portland on September 23, 2009 when you looked me in the eye and said why haven't you written it yet. There's so much that you have done for me my friend that I can't give you enough thanks in just a short section. Your never-ending support, loyalty and belief in me have allowed me to do things in my life that I hadn't imagined before our meeting.

To the incomparable Bo Eason, you taught me the power of vulnerability and story. Our friendship is one of my life's greatest blessings and you have pushed me and still do to be the best I can be. Brothers in bloodshed!

Scott Hoffman one of the best literary agents around, your wisdom and friendship is an always welcome source of peace. This book wouldn't be what it is had you not told me that day at the Sofitel to go and write the book and you wouldn't look at my book proposal. Because of you this book is nothing like what I thought I was going to write, it is much more.

To my Australian Thought Leader partners, Matt Church, Peter Cook and Scott Stein, Matt you gave me a whole new way to think and look at things, through a thought leader's mind. The support, encouragement and good old Aussie razing has raised my game and allowed to look deeper at the concepts and teachings that I was putting out there. Pete and Scott you consistently challenging me to get out there and move forward beyond my comfort zone where the real game is played.

Ah then there is Jenni Robbins, you believed in me, my mission and my message and have stood by my side to watch it come alive every step of the way. You have taught me how to create an experience through my work that transcends simply teaching.

To Denise McIntyre, you saw the potential in my message and kicked me around to make sure that I delivered with the level of excellence to make sure that my family, team and community's dreams are served at the highest level. Thanks for opening your arms to my family.

Aricia Lee you spent so many countless hours sitting in a Starbucks listening to me rant and helping me make sense of it to bring it to life on the pages here.

Gary Zamir you were my first entrepreneurial mentor and you planting the seeds in my mind of possibility that there is freedom through entrepreneurship. You taught me to look beyond the status quo and society's well-worn path to find my own way.

Steven Linder from the days we were stranded in London with 200 kids at youth camp, I have watched you dedicate yourself and sacrifice repeatedly for the greater good. You are willing to give like no one else I know and I have been the blessed beneficiary of that friendship.

To the whole team at Morgan James Publishing (Dave Hancock, Margo Toulouse, Bethany Marshall and Jim Howard), thanks for believing in this first-time author in this space and to see the big picture of what this book was about.

Gary Ericsson the founder of Clif Bar, thank you for building a company where people mattered more than profit and showing that not only is it possible it's imperative. Thanks for being willing to share your journey with me. Also,

Nido Qubein, who is a story in himself of inspiration, dedication and leadership unequaled by very many. You have always been giving and gracious to me from the day we met at my first NSA conference years ago in New Orleans.

Then there is my family that without them, this book would have no meaning. To my beautiful wife and partner in life, Stefanie you captured my heart in a moment at Gate 88 at San Francisco Airport and my life has never been the same. Thank you for loving me completely and being willing to ride this crazy ride called entrepreneurship with me. This journey would be a lonely one without you by my side. I love you my bride.

My incredible son, Jeremy, you are one my life's greatest gifts and one of my life's greatest teachers. Much of what is in these pages was my way to create a manual for you as you embark on your journey. You have inspired me to try to be an example for you to follow and to step and stand up when things were tough in spite of it all because you were worth fighting for. Thanks to Kamie for standing by your side as you grow your business and through all the creative ideas that run in your head.

And my brother, Jeff—as the song goes, you were always the wind beneath my wings. You have been the catalyst for me to go after my dreams. I couldn't ask for a better brother or friend that without knowing you pushed me to be better.

To Mom for always being the pillar of strength in our family. You and dad taught us kids that if we had the ability it is our responsibility to make a difference and help others.

My cousin Richard Ardi, where do I start — you were my first client when I started on my own and you took great joy in testing me and what I stood for. Thanks for always being there in your uniquely irritating but loving way.

FOREWORD

by Brendon Burchard

I never identified myself as an entrepreneur.

Perhaps that is why I went broke so quickly when I started my first business.

I didn't accept the identity of a risk-taker, a game-changer, a company-builder, a legacy-shaper. And so I didn't approach commerce with the kind of zeal necessary to make waves and boldly enter the unknown. I didn't try to break convention. I didn't think team and scale. I didn't envision the long-term. I faced the ultimate problem for entrepreneurs: *I let my small business make me small-minded.*

This book is a *solution* to that problem, and it's why you need to read it.

You may not know it now, but you are likely thinking too narrowly about your idea, and about business itself.

If you're just starting out, you're thinking, *Gosh, I'd love to follow my passions—hopefully things turn out and I make enough money.* You are focused on the tasks of getting started, the critics, the amount of money you have in the bank, the rent, the team, the potential customers.

If you have a growing business, you've probably been heads down, focused on your growth strategy, technology, competition, pricing models, and operational processes.

The issue is that there are bigger, more complex questions you need to focus on throughout your entrepreneurial journey, and you can never lose sight of:

- How should I *think* about success?
- How will I show up and what will I stand for every day?
- What type of company do I want to scale now?
- How should I seek to influence others?
- How will I treat employees and customers?
- How will I deal with conflict? Failure?
- How can I stay sane and be present with my family while growing this thing?
- What is my true calling?

These types of questions are like philosophical puzzles that we must piece together, break apart, and replace on a weekly basis. If unexplored, these questions will haunt entrepreneurs later in life as they watch their business fail—or, just as bad, watch their business succeed leaving a growth trail littered with failed marriages, broken promises and lost souls.

The Entrepreneurs Solution helps us tackle this grand puzzle of profit and purpose. It's a book that is ultimately about *you*, about your character and conduct. This is not another throw away book about how to form an LLC or implement the latest social media fad; this is a thesis on how to think, how to show up, and how to make your mark from one of the smartest businessmen I've ever met. That's why I'm endorsing it.

You see, as soon as you force yourself to contemplate the ideas and frameworks in this book, you'll start to think about your life and legacy with a wider, more inspired and abundant view. Even if you disregard every piece of advice in the book, and all you did was simply look at the frameworks and contemplate them deeply on your own, then you would undoubtedly find great value and transformation here.

But let me make a recommendation. Read every word of this book. It won't take long for you to realize its author, Mel Abraham, is an incredibly smart, thoughtful, successful, and conscious person. His stories and advice will focus your mind on one of life's most important questions: *Who am I, really, and what kind of life do I want to live?*

Mel and I have discussed that question in some form or another, nearly every month, for the better part of seven years. We're both blessed to be in the experts industry—sharing our advice as a profession with millions of people and with live audiences worldwide. We spend a lot of time together on the road and backstage. I've been lucky to have him speak to my audiences, and I've been blessed to present on his stages. I've done business deals with him. I've gotten to know his family well. And so I have a good idea about how he approaches life and business, and I'd like to share some things I've learned about the man. You're going to be reading his book, so you might like to know something about him.

Mel is one of the most intelligent, thoughtful, and successful people I've ever met, and not just in business. In Montana, where I was raised, we'd call him an "all-around man," meaning he's just good to the core and good at everything he does. His talents and roles are wide-ranging, a modern Renaissance man. He's a CPA; an internationally respected business valuation expert; a well-known business trainer; a black belt in multiple martial arts; a multimillionaire investor; an online educator; a profoundly caring and present father; a fun-loving and supportive husband; a trusted and close friend to nearly everyone who knows him. He's in the rare air of entrepreneurs who has achieved incredible financial freedom and at the same time a healthy lifestyle thriving with friends, family, free time, adventure, and love.

I haven't made a major business decision in the last five years without seeking Mel's advice. He's saved me from bad decisions, bad contracts, bad partnerships, and, recently, he saved me nearly half-a-million dollars in two phone calls. I've never met someone so attuned to the big picture and yet so brilliant in the details. And if you want to know the man deeply, just consider how he writes about his son in the Acknowledgments: "My incredible son, Jeremy, you are one my life's greatest gifts and one of my life's greatest teachers. Much of what is in these pages was my way to create a manual for you as you embark on your journey."

Mel goes on to describe the *Solution* this way: "This is a book about harnessing your creative force, breaking free of your former state, and getting your life in alignment with your intention and purpose." In my favorite parts of the book, you'll learn why you should "lose yourself in something that warms your heart," and the profound truth that "whenever we choose not to grow, we are working against our true nature." You'll learn the difference between getting rich and "enriching one's years and enjoying the journey." How to add value? How to think about money and partnerships? That's all here too. Most importantly, Mel will teach you all this with compassion and humanity, two things we need more of in the business world.

You're going to learn a lot in this book, and I'm excited for you. I can relate with your feelings as you start or scale your business.

I vividly remember the day I decided to start learning more about entrepreneurship—to finally start taking my new business and my life seriously, to start aligning my intentions and actions.

I was broke and living in my girlfriend's apartment. I had recently quit my corporate job to start my dream of becoming a writer and trainer. I knew nothing about running my own business. No one knew me. I didn't know how to write or publish a book. Facebook and YouTube were just a few years old. I had to teach myself to build websites and do online marketing.

Our apartment was so small that there was no room for a proper desk, so I worked and wrote on a foldout 'desk' borrowed from my mother's old sewing room. I used the bed as my extended desk, where I stacked all my bills and notes and fears.

One night, I watched my girlfriend walk into the bedroom and, trying not to disturb my papers or me, quietly slip beneath the covers. *I saw my woman sleeping under the weight of my bills.* It broke my heart.

The situation forced an all-in decision: Either I was going to become a writer and trainer and build a business doing it, getting in the game despite the uncertainty and hardship, awaking each morning to thrust my intention into the distance like a spear and seeking to reach it each day no matter the obstacle until I ended up successful... or I was going to end up with the angels for having happily exhausted myself trying to improve our lives and follow my dreams.

I decided I was not going to waste my days meandering about or marching under the banner of other people's rules;

I decided I must change the situation and follow my dreams with more focus and intensity;

I decided to fight for my art and amplify my voice into the world so that I might make a greater difference;

I decided not to worry about the critics and instead give my whole heart and effort to those who wanted positivity and progress in life;

I decided to think bigger, to overcome my fears and insecurities, to think about changing the world.

I decided to stop letting my small business make me small-minded;

I decided to marry that girl.

And that leads to today.

I'm still the same guy, driven by a fierce desire to live fully, love openly, make a difference. I still look the same, though my bad haircut now costs a bit more, and the daily activity is the same: writing, pouring out my soul, trying to figure out how to say things that help and inspire people.

All that has changed, really, is my brand business scaled immensely, even as I kept my core principles the same.

What changed are the venues and the platforms and the fans. Now I write in the library of one of my dream homes. As Facebook and YouTube grew up, so did I. As of today, 2.4 million fans follow me on Facebook, and last year alone 17,000,000 people watched my YouTube videos, making my show the most watched direct-to-camera self-help series in history. At this writing, my latest book, *The Motivation Manifesto*, is its ninth week on the *New York Times* bestseller list, my third *New York Times* bestseller in a row. My podcast debuted at #1 on iTunes in multiple countries. SUCCESS Magazine named me to their Top 25 Most Influential list along with Oprah and so many personal growth legends, and Entrepreneur rated my seminar in its Top 5 must-attends for entrepreneurs. Now I'm the highest paid motivation and high performance trainer in the world, and I share stages and swap phone calls with world leaders and innovators. And, finally, I don't have to eat cheap noodle dinners or watch my family struggle.

This all happened because I built my business thinking of the bigger picture, that puzzle I told you about, the ideas in this book. And when you do that and display that level of humanity and discipline, the market cheers you on and shares your work and products. For me, at the beginning, there were just a few fans, five or ten. And then there were fifty. Then a hundred, then a thousand, and then, as I just stayed with it for eight years every single day with full faith and joy and a dedication to excellence and service... well, here we are.

Could I have done all this without Mel Abraham in my life? Maybe. But I wouldn't have enjoyed the journey half as much or turned out to be half the man.

And so I say this to you, my friends:

Read this book and use it as a tool to think about your life.

As you begin your journey, never limit the vision you have for your life based on your current circumstances or competencies. Regardless of your past, you are more powerful, imaginative, and strong than you imagine.

I had no reason to believe that I could one day live my dream as a writer and trainer; no reason to believe, I suppose, except that my heart told me it was my path, except that my mind invented dreams that felt so real, that faith said all the struggle and the hardship and the toil would be worth it. And it was and still is. So, please, believe in your heart and your voice and your mission no matter what, no matter how small it all feels now.

Also, don't listen to the "realists" or the standard bearers of the status quo as you begin your dream. The masses confined to mediocrity will tell you to set 'smart' goals and 'play it safe' and 'await the perfect timing.' But smart goals almost always end up being weak goals, utterly predictable and absurdly measured small plans for small people who need certainty and safety to such a degree they cannot wade into the wide territory of the unknown where real vision and progress and vital entrepreneurship lives.

From my vantage point, no great innovation or human leap forward came from a predictable path or an idea that was immediately 'attainable' or 'realistic.' It's rare that these types of goals ever spark the imagination or fire the will of the human spirit. That's why we are now a culture flooded with tasks and spreadsheets and work plans that inspire no heart, no drive, no courage.

You want to change? You want a growing business? Then do not, under any circumstances, allow yourself to settle on a vision or a calling or a change in any arena that is uninspiring. If you're going to have clarity on something in your life, make it something so big and bright and meaningful that you will get out of bed and chase it until you grasp it or die. Bring forth a desire that is unbounded and even scares you a little bit, that will demand all the best that is in you, that takes you out of your own orbit and into the stratosphere of the remarkable. That kind of desire changes your life, and it changes the world.

This is the ethos that perpetuates this book, and Mel's life. He and I both believe that the journey to legend begins the moment our bias for ease and comfort is overpowered by our drive for challenge and contribution.

And so, dear Entrepreneur, keep working, keep at it, *believe*. Never forget that growth and greatness often come from those seemingly endless, fruitless days and nights of faith and discipline and service.

No matter how small you start, start something that matters.

Brendon Burchard
Founder of High Performance Academy and
New York Times bestselling author of *The Motivation Manifesto*
and *The Millionaire Messenger*

WHY CRISIS IS GOOD—MY STORY

When my son Jeremy was six, he came home from school one day and handed me a picture he had drawn that day. Here was this picture done in blue felt pen a stick figure man with dark, wavy hair standing in front of two computer screens, holding a telephone to each ear while a third phone rang on the desk. It didn't register at first. Then I realized, this was my son's impression of his dad: unsmiling and completely wired in to his technology. What an eye-opener and a dagger in the heart, Jeremy didn't have a visual of us playing ball or going to Disneyland—all he had was me at work. A real sad statement of his reality. And mine.

As a full-time single father, I had recently started my own consulting and advisory business, so a lot of my days were spent at my home office on the phone with clients, dealing with valuation matters, focusing on doing business deals, building businesses, and litigation. It was something of a scramble to penetrate this competitive field and position myself effectively in it, so I was also speaking all over the country and doing what I could to make it all work. Most days, though, I would pick Jeremy up from my parents' house after work, cook us dinner, spend some precious time with him before putting him to bed, then go back to my home office to work. I spent most nights poring over hundreds of pages of documents.

My son's drawing hit me right between the eyes and directly in the heart with just how much of my life was consumed by work. Though I didn't change my workaholic habits overnight, at least I was aware of them. I knew that Jeremy was watching me . . . and learning based on what he saw. I began to question how or if it possible to live my dream while taking care of my life's most precious gift, my son. I imagined a life where both could coexist, my entrepreneurial dream and a caring, loving and deep relationship with my son.

When Jeremy was sixteen, he was spending a lot of time on the computer himself, playing online games and searching the Web. I wanted him to know that he could apply his passion in positive and productive ways, so I got him a domain based on his name, and some software he could use to learn to create his own website. He enjoyed it so much, it became the birth of his own business: building websites for other companies. When Father's Day came around that year, he was away at football camp, so he e-mailed me a photo. It showed a father and son walking hand in hand on the beach at sunset, with a quote from Clarence Budington Kelland: *"He didn't tell me how to live; he lived, and let me watch him do it."* At the bottom, Jeremy thanked me for everything I had ever done for him, including getting him a new car.

Then one morning three years later, on my way to the gym, life came into quick focus when my shoelace got caught in my mountain bike chain as I was going about twenty-five miles per hour downhill. I had been angry that morning and preoccupied with thoughts of the person who brought on the anger, so I was not paying much attention to trivial details such as shoelaces. Maybe that's why it's called "blind rage."

It happened in a split second. I was zipping downhill one moment and flying through the air the next. I landed headfirst on the concrete. Even in a helmet, the impact knocked me senseless and left me with a grade-four concussion and a dislocated shoulder. A nurse who happened to be driving by saw the accident and stopped to help me. I could move, but I had no sensation on the right side of my body. While I was being taped onto a body board in the back of the ambulance, slipping in and out of consciousness on my way to the emergency room, I kept asking myself, *Did I spend my time on the right things? Did I teach Jeremy what matters most? Do I even know what that is?*

Meanwhile, Jeremy, nineteen by then, was sending a text: "If this is the end, I only hope my dad knows how much I love him."

It shifted everything: my values, our relationship, my plans for the future. Regaining consciousness in the hospital, I started to wonder, *have I given my son the tools he needs to live the life he wants—the life he deserves?* I knew he would be set for life financially if, God forbid, something did happen to me, but I didn't want him to wait another thirty years to understand the difference between wealth and fulfillment. There was "getting rich," and then there was enriching one's years and enjoying the journey. I wanted him to enjoy the journey.

My doctors told me that most people don't walk away from an accident like this. But for the helmet and my level of fitness, I would have ended up in a wheelchair—or a body bag. My doctors said I would need six to nine months to resume normal functioning. But I was motivated—I wanted the chance to teach my son something more significant than whatever he had managed to learn from me so far. After Jeremy promised the doctors he would watch me around the clock, I returned home within a few days and powered through my rehabilitation. Within three months, I could move my limbs, but still I had no feeling on the right side, and my speech was slurred. Trying to communicate was frustrating. It also made working virtually impossible because my business relied so much on my ability to communicate. But this proved to be a blessing in disguise, because it freed up my time and forced me to be introspective.

I had mentored my son for the past four years as he grew his own business. Well, good for us, but *had I taught him how to live a courageous life, the same way my father had taught me: by example? Did he know how to be happy and live life on his own terms?* Wanting to convey to Jeremy my regrets over the past as well as my excitement for the future, I started to write a journal. The process proved invaluable.

I started writing down the traits and strategies I had learned from the pivotal experiences in fulfilling my own aspirations. Over the previous twenty-five years, I had grown several of my own successful businesses, including litigation and consulting firms. I had become a strategic consultant and adviser to numerous businesses, entrepreneurs, and executives and had gotten tremendous results. I had served as an expert witness in valuation cases around the country and sat on the boards of directors of several companies, including one that we took from $40 million to over $250 million in ten years. And once I lost a full third of my net worth because of a bad decision but then rebuilt it, quadrupling my earlier success. While all this represented a life well lived, I felt a pull to make an even greater difference in my son's life. More than my wealth, Jeremy needed my wealth of *knowledge*. He would soon graduate from college with a BA in business. But what would that get him, really?

He and his friends were entering a job market that was, for the most part, not hiring. Their generation had grown up inside a bubble that burst just as they were preparing to enter the workforce. It was a big mess made by the same folks who had been telling their kids their whole lives, "If you make a mess, you've got to clean it up." Now the kids found themselves in the position of having to clean up their parents' financial and environmental messes. But what kinds of skills had they been taught? *Did this new generation know how to make their own success when it wasn't handed to them? Had they ever been given the chance to develop the innovative thinking skills they now needed to navigate a shifting job market?*

Their models for success growing up were dot-coms that gained overnight success with little more than a domain name, and rock star billionaires (some of them notorious college dropouts), who made it all look so easy. Of course, many of the dot-coms proved unsustainable because they had no foundation beneath them, and the immense success of companies such as Google and Facebook were the exception, not the rule.

Then, in an increasingly competitive environment, they were told that scoring high on tests and getting straight A's was the goal. From junior high school onward, their sole focus was getting into a good college, as if their future depended on it. And yet, studies showed that the kids who finally did get into that good college were already burned out and stressed out from pushing so hard for so long. As a result, they were studying less and partying more, as if they had already reached the finish line. It made me wonder what they were going to do when the race really started and they were on their own. *Did they know what it was like to achieve something great because their own passion compelled them? Or how fulfilling it is to turn an idea into a profitable venture that helps other people?* As far as I could tell, they had very little time or support to be innovative and resourceful, discover their own creative problem-solving abilities, or test out their entrepreneurial ideas—because none of those critical life skills were quantifiable enough to be measured by a grade. And yet, these were the very inner resources they now needed to pull themselves up by their bootstraps and rise to the challenges in front of them.

There are many ways to rise to the challenges we face together, and an entrepreneurial mind-set encompasses them all. All business skills are learnable. And the best businesses have more far-reaching objectives than "I'll get mine; you get yours." As I wrote through the pain and headaches of my recovery, I watched millions of workers get laid off from their jobs, lose their homes in foreclosure, and seek government assistance. My sense of urgency to finish this book grew. Meanwhile, the country, too, was going through a recovery of its own, and the prognosis for *when* either of us would land back on our feet again was undetermined. I started to interview CEOs of companies that were faring well amid the storm, to find out what was keeping them afloat and on course, and how they had persevered through challenges in the past. And I have included their hard-won wisdom in this book. Their stories supported the very framework for sustainable success that I had used in my own businesses and the businesses I worked with over the years. The framework requires simply the mastery of the four areas of business that form the solid foundation of all sustainable and successful companies: **Mind-set, Marketing, Mechanics,** and **Money.** This model has become known as the Business Mastery Blueprint.™

BUSINESS MASTERY BLUEPRINT™

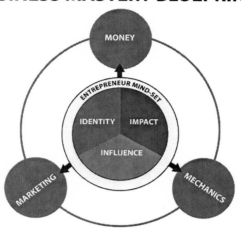

The three elements *marketing, mechanics,* and *money* are the obvious suspects, right? But it's the least obvious one—*mind-set*—that is actually most important. You will see from this book that mind-set is the basis for the other three: marketing, mechanics, and money. All great companies and brilliant ideas originated in someone's mind. For us to grow anything positive, prosperous, and sustainable, the proper nutrients must be in place in our thinking processes. The richer the soil, the better the results. Anyone can have a great idea for a product or service, but it's what happens afterward that matters most. Only 4 percent of these innovators hang in there long enough to sustain their business idea beyond ten years. It's those 4 percent who know how to connect with people, seize opportunity, manage conflict, approach decisions, deal with stress, seek to serve, and create a team around their values. All this determines a leader. And the leadership mind-set in turn determines the company culture, branding, customer relationships, team cohesion, and, ultimately, market viability. These all arise from having systems in place that make the company expandable and scalable (mechanics), effective ways to connect with your greater community (marketing), and a sustainable financial plan that generates profit (money). That is the **Business Mastery Blueprint**.™

The biggest gift that came out of my bicycle accident was the realization that I had regrets. This brought my priorities and purpose into clear focus. My passion returned, my progress accelerated, and my health, my business, and my relationships all improved. In a best-case scenario, crisis awakens our senses and clarifies our desires. Our national economic crisis can serve the same purpose. We have the opportunity to reassess our priorities and use our circumstances as an opportunity to discover what we are really made of. Rather than wait out a period of struggle and hardship only to return to "business as usual," we can innovate more stable and sustainable ways of doing business. We have all the inner resources we need to rise to the occasion. We need only to harness the entrepreneurial mind. And on the other side of that is a land where your team is connected, committed and loyal. Your customers become raving fans and your life full with fulfillment because the business you are creating is in congruence with your values, operated in alignment with your higher vision and connected to all stakeholders at an emotional level. As a result, your business serves them by transforming their lives. All of this will translate into more profits, fans and freedom. Welcome to *The Entrepreneur's Solution*.

CHAPTER 1

INTRODUCING . . . [*DRUMROLL*]

THE ENTREPRENEUR'S SOLUTION

Sir Richard Branson once said, "Entrepreneurship is the golden highway to economic freedom, plus it's an exciting and fun way to make a living." And I agree with him. The solutions to our nation's issues and flagging spirits are going to be not *political* but *entrepreneurial* solutions. Today, perhaps more than ever, is the time for you, the new entrepreneur, to take responsibility for the future and improve on it. The new entrepreneurs are passionate enough to try new solutions to age-old problems. They make it their mission to make a positive difference in people's lives. And in the process of striving to reach their own potential, they discover new, ingenious ways to benefit entire communities, whether local or global, through their success.

The choices we make today will create our tomorrow. It's time we chose what we really want and what we want to pass along to our children. When I talk about this, it is not simply about passing along wealth, riches, or "stuff";

it is about passing along values, skills, culture, philosophy, and the necessary resources to thrive for generations to come.

During these past three decades—the luxury-obsessed eighties, the bloated nineties, and this most recent clamor for quick Wall Street money—we lost sight of our search for a meaningful and fulfilling existence. We got complacent. We got caught up in consuming rather than creating. Having possessions was more important than having passion. And yet, 80 percent [1] of all Americans will retire financially dependent on the government, family, or charity. A total of 40 percent[2] are not putting any money way for retirement. As of 2012, as much as 50 percent[3] of families in the United States spend more than they earn on credit cards, debt, and mortgages, and will spend what was supposed to be their retirement years just trying to *retire* their debt. The figure is probably higher now.

Our human potential is much greater than that! The only way to find out just *how* great we can be is to take an entrepreneurial approach to our future, as Americans did in the past. The entrepreneurial spirit has always been one of our great traits. It is our innately innovative problem-solving ability that has gotten us through setbacks before, and it will again. The attributes of *The Entrepreneur's Solution* are timeless, and now they are especially timely.

Although we have seen an increase in the number of self-employed Americans from nine million in 2009 to fourteen million in 2010, we have seen a corresponding decrease since then to approximately ten million[4] today. That is almost a one-third decrease in entrepreneurs. It is likely that a large percentage of these are part of the new breed of "necessity entrepreneurs," who plowed the last of their savings into one good idea because it seemed their only option but did not have the tools, training or skills to make it a success. So I wrote this book for those newly self-employed, who may or may not know what it takes to determine their own fate. I wrote for the recently "downsized" out of a job and for the baby boomers who would need other sources of income during their

---

1   http://www.statisticbrain.com/retirement-statistics/
2   http://www.statisticbrain.com/retirement-statistics/
3   http://www.huffingtonpost.com/2012/05/17/americans-spending-more-than-they-earn_n_1523920.html
4   http://www.careerbuilder.com/share/aboutus/pressreleasesdetail.aspx?sd=2%2F6%2F2014&id=pr802&ed=12%2F31%2F2014

increasingly uncertain "retirement years." I wrote it for all those who plot an escape from their jobs every day yet are made to feel that they'd better be grateful for what they have no matter how unhappy it makes them. And I wrote it for Jeremy and the rest of that young generation, to walk them through the process of turning latent potential into the fulfillment of their dreams.

I wrote *The Entrepreneur's Solution* to answer the questions we are asking ourselves today and the ones we should continue asking ourselves tomorrow: *What will it take for us to prosper? How do we stop this backward slide into debt and despair? And how can we build businesses based on broader ideals that prosper everyone?* This country was built on principles of entrepreneurialism, equity, self-determinism, and opportunity. Fulfilling our potential, as individuals and as a nation, is simply a matter then of reawakening that innate spirit. We have a unique opportunity to reinvent ourselves today. In fact, it's already happening.

The New Entrepreneur

In my research for this book, I was heartened to discover that millions of Americans were already shifting their priorities. More entrepreneurship clubs in universities, and college courses on entrepreneurship were springing up. More college graduates than ever were spending a year or more working within social entrepreneurial organizations, not just for the experience but because the new entrepreneur genuinely seeks to bring more consciousness into business and to have a positive effect in the world she or he has inherited.

Today's entrepreneurs are a "leaner, meaner" bunch, forging sustainable ways of doing business. They steer away from the old business-as-usual model to find instead ways to connect, collaborate, and contribute. Perhaps because of the nature of technology, they are more flexible, in-the-moment decision makers. The new entrepreneurs live in the here and now while scaling their businesses for future expansion. This holistic approach seeks sustainable solutions.

The new entrepreneurial mind of the twenty-first century stimulates the imagination. Its stories provide the kind of inspiration we all need to thrive again. Lessons from today's most enterprising and socially conscious CEOs appear throughout each chapter to demonstrate what it takes to build profitable, responsible companies.

As we examine these successes, some common themes emerge. New entrepreneurs . . .

- monetize what is most meaningful to them
- are fulfilled to the extent that they are spending their lives in pursuit of their dreams
- make a concerted effort to balance work with their preferred lifestyle
- do not delay rewards and enjoyment until retirement
- are as values-driven as they are profit-driven
- do well by doing good

Though the CEOs I interviewed and researched all had very different personalities and backgrounds, they shared some of the same attitudes and habits that helped me in my own business and in various consulting assignments. They all had similar stories about the thrills and challenges of taking a new enterprise to the top:

- what it took to turn an idea into a moneyed venture
- what inspired them to keep overcoming the odds
- how they managed unmanageable people
- how they grew when others were falling on hard times
- how they maintained their values in a tough, competitive environment
- how they sustained growth while maintaining their core values
- what made them stand out above the rest
- how they balanced work with family life and pleasure

The Business Mastery Blueprint™

Based on our common experiences, I figured there were already enough hyped-up books in the business section, selling their systems for acquiring luxury real estate and going it alone while screwing the competition. In contrast, this holistic entrepreneurial model is not based on greed, yet it supports our pursuit of happiness and prosperity. I call it *sustainable success* because it is based on the creatively adaptable mind that can learn to survive and thrive in good times and bad.

BUSINESS MASTERY BLUEPRINT™

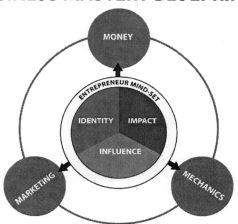

Ask anyone who owns and operates a business—it's a balancing act. You have the *mechanics*. This is all the legal and organizational stuff that goes into building it. It is effectively about the roles and rules. Then you have the *marketing*, which means you have to find a way to engage and enroll others in your vision, then connect with your customers in a meaningful enough way to keep them coming back. This is effectively about connecting and communicating. To understand what motivates your market to buy, you first need to understand how the mind operates. Then, of course, there's the *money*—or not, depending on how good you are at getting it, keeping it, investing it, and getting more of it. This is effectively about the flows and the financials.

Meanwhile, our *mind-set* remains the foundation for all the rest. As your own boss, each day you will need to make hundreds of decisions, manage relationships, manage your emotions and fears, navigate through confusion, get past any tendency to procrastinate, balance your personal and professional priorities, and understand what your target market really needs. *How will you balance making money with the other areas of your life that you value? How will you make your offer, product, or message meaningful to those you most want it to reach? How will you find the right partners to collaborate with? How will you overcome daily challenges and "personal overwhelm"? And where will you find the courage to begin all these things NOW?*

The answers to these questions lie primarily in the one element of the blueprint that permeates all the others: *mind-set.* It is both the soil and the soul from which all ideas gestate and grow.

So Let's Till the Soil

NINE ENTREPRENEURIAL ESSENTIALS ™

Building a business over time takes an enormous amount of mental agility, emotional resilience, and even physical stamina. The Nine Entrepreneurial Essentials that make up the three elements of mind-set encompass it all. Each of the three elements corresponds to one of the three parts of this book, and each part will take you systematically through the three Entrepreneurial Essentials that make up that element. Each essential is actually a prescriptive transition necessary to shift your mind-set from one quadrant to another in the process model. For instance, someone who falls in the Creative Saboteur quadrant typically has lots of ideas and is constantly coming up with more. The challenge at this level is that Creative Saboteurs typically do not stay on one track long enough for any idea to gain market traction. By working through the building blocks described in this book, you begin to shift your mind-set "up and right" to that of the Entrepreneurial Superstar. We will discuss this process model and the prescriptive transitions in greater depth later in the book, after we've discussed the various elements and building blocks of the model itself.

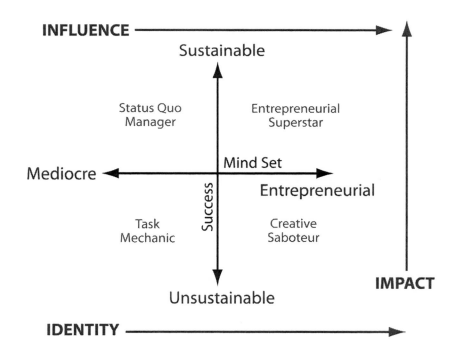

There are plenty of ways to make money that work great in the short term but simply are not sustainable in the long term. The challenge is to be profitable in a way that is both achievable in the short term and sustainable in the long term. This means that we need to consider tomorrow in all our business practices today. And it's going to take a whole lot of entrepreneurial ingenuity, as well as *clarity, courage,* and *character.* The new entrepreneur will also need to find new ways to *connect* and *collaborate* with others, so we can *capitalize* on more sustainable values. In other words, we need to implement business models that generate profit by supporting life.

The new entrepreneur will also need the ability to *commit* to his or her core values and dreams, to *create* community and a corporate culture, and, ultimately, to *contribute* something that can continue to grow and that benefits the many and not just the few.

So How Does All This Work?

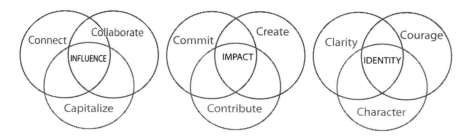

These elements create a system for the entrepreneurial mind-set and sustainable success that is not necessarily chronological in its application. A book, however, best serves its reader by conveying its message in a certain order. So the chapters are organized around your developing each of the Nine Entrepreneurial Essentials sequentially. Each of the nine essential traits is made up of two building blocks. For example, to gain *clarity* requires both *focus* and *vision*. To *connect* with others, we need to develop both *empathy* and *communication* skills. This is how we progress from conception of a business idea, through the stages of ideation, to germination and, finally, fruition.

This doesn't mean you can't also open straight to any chapter and work on your weakest point, or target whatever you need to strengthen in the moment to deal with a current situation. Each chapter will give you a fundamental understanding of the two building blocks of each element. Then you will be given direction on how to assess your location within the quadrant. This will allow you to work through the prescriptive transitions, moving from one quadrant to another, and to achieve sustainable success with an entrepreneurial mind-set.

I do suggest that you learn the material as if you were going to be teaching it. That's the most efficient way to incorporate the knowledge. And the fact is, you *will* want to teach it to people in your company, as well as to others who share your objectives. Getting the whole team thinking on the same page has a ripple effect that will augment every aspect of your company.

The new entrepreneurial mind approaches success with the understanding that an entrepreneur's values and business decisions not only reflect in the company's profit and longevity; they also have an impact within the company's community, be it local or global. So the process begins with some introspection. Part One, "Identity," develops the core inner strengths of *clarity, courage,* and *character,* which are needed before you can grow your idea, product, or service in the world.

Part Two, "Influence," is all about mastering the fuzzy science: people. Success is always a collaboration. It's imperative that you enter into the hearts and minds of your market—to communicate, negotiate, manage, send a message, understand your own decision-making process, and maintain dominion in other crucial areas of your business where ego and emotions can and will get involved. This section will teach you how to empathize with and engage your market, coworkers, partners, capital investors, family members, and anyone else you rely on for the company's success. This is accomplished through the all-important ability to *connect, collaborate,* and *capitalize* on your product/service, image, reputation, public perception,

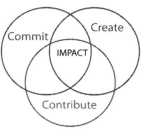

and everything else of value that you create.

Part Three, "Impact" will have you expanding your business to make your market presence felt and experienced by the many rather than the few. This is where the entrepreneur's ability to *commit, create,* and *contribute* comes into play in actualizing your higher potential and that of the company. Make your success as big as you want. Master this realm to expand your company and affect your culture, not only locally but globally.

Because what if, in the end, making money isn't actually the be-all and end-all to living a great, fulfilling existence? What if it's the other way around: that fulfilling your potential is the means to creating more wealth? *The Entrepreneur's Solution* dismantles almost everything you ever learned growing up about "making a living," so that you can have a life. I'm not saying it's going to be easy. I am saying it's going to be exciting and fulfilling. So dust off those dreams. Together, we are going to turn your potential into a profitable, thriving company. And I mean business!

> To access free training and more resources go to:
> **www.theentrepreneurssolution.com/resources**

Harness the New Entrepreneurial Mind

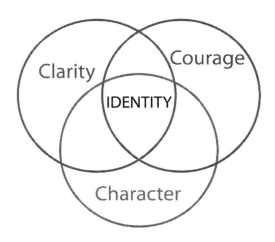

An entrepreneur's identity always reflects in his or her business. In this first section, you will delve inward and discover how your thinking establishes a pattern of either success or failure. You will learn techniques to take charge of your mental and emotional states. Ultimately, this identity will become your business philosophy, your company culture, and your brand. And it will happen naturally, through your understanding of the first three essentials and their respective building blocks of **clarity** (focus and vision), **courage** (confidence and responsibility), and **character** (conviction and action).

CHAPTER 2

THE DIFFERENCE BETWEEN COOKING AN EGG AND POWERING A CITY

The world demands the qualities of youth: not the time of life but a state
of mind, a temper of will, a quality of the imagination, a predominance of
courage over timidity, of the appetite for adventure over the love of ease.
—Robert F. Kennedy

Electrical power plants are powered by steam—water vapor. If you've ever seen Niagara Falls or the Grand Canyon, you know what water can accomplish. But *steam*? Yes, the stuff that wafts off your coffee in the morning. Harness enough of it, and you can power a city. Now picture an egg. Water will boil it. That's great—I appreciate a good boiled egg once in a while. Then what's the difference between cooking that egg and powering a whole city? Between hot water and steam? One degree. As the temperature rises that last degree to around 212, the water molecules accelerate just enough to break free from their liquid state and turn a power plant turbine or send a steam locomotive roaring down the track.

That one-degree makes all the difference in your business. That's the power of the entrepreneurial spirit to expand and accelerate your success. And that's the transformation you can experience as you learn each aspect of the Nine Entrepreneurial Essentials of *The Entrepreneur's Solution*. Make that one-degree shift, and you can move the world with the impact of your ideas. Harness your latent power, and you can carry yourself and others to the far reaches of your imagination.

This is a book about harnessing your creative force, breaking free of your former state, and getting your life in alignment with your intention and purpose.

Putting each of the Nine Entrepreneurial Essentials into practice, you will develop, among other skills, the flexibility, strength, and character to power through anything.

If you are currently struggling in an existing business, you can use this Business Mastery Blueprint™ to turn your challenges into opportunities for growth and innovate ways to expand your company's impact in the marketplace. If you are new to the game and hoping to get a business idea off the ground, you can use the Business Mastery Blueprint™ to grow your skills and your idea through every phase, from germination to fruition. The effectiveness of your *marketing, mechanics,* and *money* strategies will be a direct result of developing the proper mind-set. It's the one piece of your business that cannot be delegated. It's the one degree of acceleration you need to fulfill your potential.

Breaking Away From the Model of Mediocrity

This one-degree transformation also represents the shift we need to make as a country: from a model of mediocrity, generated by societal norms, to a new paradigm of *sustainable success;* from living on autopilot and just getting by to finding out what we are truly capable of, so that we can thrive together, living and prospering at our full potential.

The upside of losing a job, along with security, status, possessions, and everything else we thought defined us, is that we are now motivated. Under this heat and pressure, we are being forced to expand beyond what we thought we were capable of. Rather than sit back and wait for fortune to come to us, we have to use every talent we have, and *create* our fortune. The loss and lack of options frees us up to finally pursue those dreams we left stashed away in the back of our mind years ago. This is the time when we can discover that we are more than what society or history has painted us to be. Breaking away from a long-accepted model of mediocrity—what I call the "old school of thought"—will move us toward our own creation of *sustainable success.*

The Old School of Thought

We live in a culture that encourages us to stay within an acceptable average called "the norm." It's not news that the average education and cultural mind-set has come to encourage conformity rather than ingenuity. The workaday world generally thwarts people's natural instinct to grow or explore new ideas. And there is a mistaken cultural notion that says being an entrepreneur is a risky choice. The reality is that without planning, all endeavors involve some degree of risk. But if you are living a risk-averse life, you probably are not living the life you want and could have.

Here are your alternatives. If life were a buffet, what would you choose off the menu?

The Model of Mediocrity	The New Entrepreneurial Mind
Struggles from day to day	Thrives in the moment
Spends as if there were no tomorrow	Invests in the future
Never sure what she or he wants	Has clarity of vision
Worries about the future	Lives for today
Procrastinates when it comes to dreams	Takes decisive action
Avoids failure	Banks on success
Takes what comes	Does whatever it takes
Clocks out at the end of the day	Commits to persevering
Perceives others as potential threats	Connects well with others
Lives for a better day	Enjoys the journey
Remains unfulfilled	Follows own heart
Job seeker	Seeks fulfillment

Tragically, the vast majority lower their own standards to avoid straying outside the mean. And if the social norm were not enough to pull us down, we are susceptible to the same pressures, or worse, from within our own families—from those who, in their own way, love us most.

I own a popular karate studio in my community. It exists to develop young minds as much as to teach martial arts. My staff and I get immense joy from watching our students grow on many levels. So it was disturbing to hear this story from one of our students, who had spent the past eight years working with famed former UCLA basketball coach John Wooden, speaking to kids at various high schools about keeping their lives on track with a good work ethic. She met a girl from a financially disadvantaged but close family, who worked so hard for her grades that she earned the opportunity to go to college. Eventually accepted at a university out of state, the young woman was proud to be the first member of her family who would go to college. Though she would have to leave home to attend this particular school and must work two jobs to pay her way, she was willing to do both. She was excited at the chance to break the cycle of disadvantage and lack of education.

As she was preparing for this next phase of her life, her mother came to her and said, "Why can't you go find a husband to take care of you, and just have babies with him, like I did?" It was the classic "if it was good enough for me, it should be good enough for you" line.

Then the mother took it one step further. Instead of supporting and encouraging her daughter, she gave her an ultimatum. She told her daughter, "If you choose to go and do this, you're not welcome back."

Needless to say, the daughter was torn. She had worked hard her whole life for this very day. And suddenly, living the life she intended came down to a choice between her family and her own fulfillment. Though it is extreme, I use this compelling story as an example of what we all face when we branch out on our own, whether to start our own business or in some way take a different track from the one expected of us.

I never did find out the end to that story. I certainly hope she made the choice to go to college, and let her mother learn her own lessons. I also use this story to show why defining your own identity for yourself will be one of the first steps you take in defining your destiny within the Business Mastery Blueprint™. You see, if this girl was raised to be "the good daughter," it would be especially challenging now to envision herself as the successful career woman. It would be incongruent with her self-perception. She would ask herself what mattered to her most, and feel a conflict that would disable her ability to move forward. I read in a recent article that one the biggest regrets that people have as they get to their waning years is that they didn't have the courage to live the life they wanted to versus following society's path of mediocrity.

Whenever we choose not to grow, we are working against our true nature. It's like holding our foot on the brake of a high-powered machine that's built for acceleration—our mind. We eventually burn out and experience the pain of regret.

Unfortunately, all this is perfectly normal. Not all of us have manipulative parents, yet we all experience pressures to "stick with what you know" and not venture too far from the norm. When a country's workforce stops reaching for its potential, it is left tired, bored, unsatisfied, and holding someone else responsible for its well-being and its next paycheck. When this mentality pervades a company or a country, it sinks the income-earning potential, as well as the creative potential, to its lowest common denominator, badly hurting the bottom line.

Settle for Nothing Less Than Sustainable Success

There is nothing wrong with having a paycheck and a little peace of mind. The problem is what we *settle* for. Our potential as a nation and as individuals is so much greater. And success is much more than a spreadsheet and a business plan.

We need only that one-degree difference, and changes for the better will be dramatic. The significance of that one degree is made clear when you consider that if a plane flying from Los Angeles to New York is off course by one degree, it can end up in Jacksonville, Florida. So don't underestimate the long-term impact of your actions and decisions today. Grasp the power you have to set yourself on a course today and get where you want to go tomorrow. Realize the ability we have as individuals to influence and change our world.

Turn Up the Heat One Degree

Capitalism is reborn in recessions and during times of economic change. The entrepreneurial spirit is the phoenix that rises from a depression or recession to save the day. How can we break away from the model of mediocrity? We need to be unreasonable again, by setting unreasonable standards for ourselves and then living by them!

We must go through our own personal reevaluations and be self-referential enough to know what we want. We must set goals that seem beyond our reach. Our road to fulfillment is paved with challenges and personal growth. There's no way around it—and that's the good news.

Businesses must be for profit. And yet,
to be sustainable, profit must be for a purpose.

The Mind-Set Behind the Methodology

Here are a few marks of the successful entrepreneur. Think about to what extent you already have these qualities, and start to imagine how you could put them into practice again:

1. Be Self-Referential

The most successful entrepreneurs ignore their critics. Start by being more self-referential—listen to your instincts more than you listen to what other people think you are capable of. Later, you will learn how to build confidence by being self-validating, too. But for now, turn your questioning inward and consider yourself the authority. Billionaires from Ted Turner to Jeff Bezos of Amazon seek advice, yet they are, at their core, self-referential. They follow their heart, and if anyone tells them they can't do something, they make it their business to prove them wrong—not just out of ego, but because their mind is telling them something different.

Early in high school, my football coach told me I was never going to be good enough to play varsity. By my senior year, I was a starter for the varsity team. When I was interested in track, the same coach told me I was never going to be a good pole-vaulter. I broke the school record by my senior year and was the top in the city that year, vaulting over fourteen feet. During my senior year in college, I was taking eighteen units when I decided to take the CPA exam before I graduated. Very few pass the exam on their first try, let alone while they are still in school. Once I decided to do it, though, I was committed. I spent a whole month in the library, studying day in and day out. By the time I graduated I had passed all four parts of the exam—on the first try, while still in college.

That kind of unwillingness to take no for an answer is part of the entrepreneurial spirit. Initially, my motivation came from not wanting to live within other people's low expectations, so I pushed myself hard. At some point, I formed my own high standards that I wanted to live up to, and those aspirations pulled me forward.

Other people's opinions of you may pose the first threat to your progress. You have to ask yourself, though, *am I willing to put on the jacket that society tells me to wear? Or am I going to be the person who raises the bar?*

2. Be Committed in the Face of Challenges

Commitment in the face of challenges is another hallmark of the successful entrepreneur. This is the only way you can influence others. The first job I got out of school was with the accounting firm Peat Marwick. One of my first assignments there was to inventory a manure company . . . in August, in Los Angeles, in 103 degrees. I didn't yet know my ultimate life purpose, but I was pretty sure it wasn't spending days surrounded by tons of steaming manure. But I also recognized that the essential skills I was learning were going to serve me for the long term as the building blocks of my career. I knew that the job would serve my greater purpose, whatever that was, so I stuck it out until I sensed I had learned what I needed to learn from it. The experience served me well because I had the persistence that I would need in my own business someday.

Skill sets are learned, but the *mind*-set is cultivated over time. When women come to my karate studio to learn self-defense, often they ask me, "How long will it take me to learn self-defense?"

I say, "I can teach you the techniques in a couple of hours. But it's the psychology to use them effectively and under stress that takes a while. Consistent practice and time gets you in the right mind-set to actually use the skills when you're under pressure."

They don't truly get what I mean until they come to class. They learn each skill fairly quickly, then drill until they feel confident enough to demonstrate the same routine set of self-defense moves. Then the day arrives when the trainers take them by surprise, escalating the level of attack by acting as pseudo attackers to authentically simulate what the student would feel on the street. When the emotions and stress rise, in many cases the skills go right out the window. Sensing real danger, the students' heart rate accelerates, and they lose the ability to think as clearly. It takes constant repetition to establish the mind-set. This process is called *stress inoculation*. The more you repeat and begin to live by the principles of *The Entrepreneur's Solution*, the more you will have a systematic, ingrained response to the stresses of entrepreneurship, with more predictable positive outcomes.

Most start-ups make the mistake of running their business tactically only. Learning basic operations, knowing how to do a spreadsheet or put together a basic website or marketing campaign—these techniques will get you only so far. Practicing the mind-set will prepare you for the unexpected, so you can still think strategically under pressure.

Sir Richard Branson may be an adventurer who thrives on adrenaline, but he is also a strategist. He gets a big idea; then he looks at it from every angle and takes time to develop it. By and large, the most successful entrepreneurs are risk evaluators. They don't just jump into risky ventures on a whim and a prayer. The new entrepreneurs have the ability to mitigate risk by doing a financial analysis of their idea. They weigh how much risk they can manage, against potential profits. Then they mitigate what risk exists, while increasing profit sources. From the outside, they may appear to be flying without a parachute. But they have developed a level of mastery over their fears, and commitment in the face of challenges. Successful serial entrepreneurs also have as many alternative plans for making it work as James Bond has gadgets for getting out of any mess.

It's shocking how many good ideas never come to fruition as a viable business because the start-up had only one plan. When it didn't work, the would-be entrepreneur gave up. And it's not always for lack of financial resources; more often, it's for lack of *inner resourcefulness*. The root of all riches lies in the mind. So this is where we will take you, right to the heart of success: your mind. Here is where your journey begins.

3. Choose

It all begins with a choice. The choice to branch out on your own is a very personal decision. It can be as simple as following an idea, yet it can prove life changing—and, potentially, culture changing. This is where you enter the realm of having an *impact*.

You have your own unique factors to consider: you could be strapped with student loans or you could have a less-than-satisfying but good-paying job. You could be responsible for a large extended family, or you could be a single mother on welfare. Whatever your age or stage in life, a new business begins with a choice, followed by a few small steps.

Here is what Jeff Bezos has to say about how one small and exciting idea germinated and grew in his mind until it became a life choice that grew into a culture-changing company called Amazon:

I got the idea to start Amazon 16 years ago. I came across the fact that Web usage was growing at 2,300 percent per year. I'd never seen or heard of anything that grew that fast, and the idea of building an online bookstore with millions of titles—something that simply couldn't exist in the physical world—was very exciting to me. I had just turned 30 years old, and I'd been married for a year. I told my wife, MacKenzie, that I wanted to quit my job and go do this crazy thing that probably wouldn't work, since most startups don't, and I wasn't sure what would happen after that. MacKenzie told me I should go for it. As a young boy, I'd been a garage inventor. I'd invented an automatic gate closer out of cement-filled tires, a solar cooker that didn't work very well out of an umbrella and tinfoil, baking-pan alarms to entrap my siblings. I'd always wanted to be an inventor, and she wanted me to follow my passion.

I decided I had to give it a shot. I didn't think I'd regret trying and failing. And I suspected I would always be haunted by a decision to not try at all. After much consideration, I took the less safe path to follow my passion, and I'm proud of that choice.

Tomorrow, in a very real sense, your life—the life you author from scratch on your own—begins.

How will you use your gifts? What choices will you make?

Will inertia be your guide, or will you follow your passions?

Will you follow dogma, or will you be original?

Will you choose a life of ease or a life of service and adventure?

Will you wilt under criticism, or will you follow your convictions?

Will you bluff it out when you're wrong, or will you apologize?

Will you guard your heart against rejection, or will you act when you fall in love?

Will you play it safe, or will you be a little bit swashbuckling?

When it's tough, will you give up, or will you be relentless?

Will you be a cynic, or will you be a builder?

Will you be clever at the expense of others, or will you be kind?

I will hazard a prediction. When you are 80 years old, and in a quiet moment of reflection narrating for only yourself the most personal version of your life story, the telling that will be most compact and meaningful will be the series of choices you have made. In the end, we are our choices. Build yourself a great story.

Build Yourself a Great Success Story and a Phenomenal Company

The questions Jeff Bezos poses reflect the alternatives you are given every day to choose between living a life of compromise and one of fulfillment. Obviously, he chose the latter for himself. It's time to make your own choices.

Answer all Jeff Bezos's questions before moving forward. Based on these answers, what one action step can you take now that will set your course in motion? When will you complete it?

To access free training and more resources go to:

www.theentrepreneurssolution.com/resources

CHAPTER 3

FOCUS: THE RIGHT ENTREPRENEURIAL STUFF

Stop asking if the glass is half full or half empty. Instead ask,
"What's in it? How did it get there? What can I do with it?"
—David Kaufman

CLARITY = Focus + Vision

C larity comes from having both *focus* in the present and *vision* for the future.

Focus is your ability to direct your mind's attention, to have your mind in the game, to "clear your headspace" so you can make good decisions in every moment.

Vision is your ability to create a bigger picture of what you want, based on your deeper values, long-term goals, and sense of greater purpose.

Possessing both focus and vision gives you the clarity to focus on the task at hand, based on your higher intentions for your future. As an entrepreneur, your focus could be on company profits, while your vision is to fulfill a higher purpose. You need focus to take immediate action, and vision to keep in mind the needs of those who work for you as you set your action plan. We use both every day when we drive—we monitor our position in relation to where we ultimately intend to go, while simultaneously adjusting our steering in the moment. Clarity is knowing exactly where you want to go and what you need to do to get there. Maintaining this level of clarity will remain your number one entrepreneurial skill.

The Entrepreneurial Mind at Work

Have you ever seen the film *Apollo 13*? My son and I love that film. We've watched it several times, and each time it is amazing to consider the challenges those three astronauts and their NASA mission support team faced during those last fateful hours of their trip to the moon.

They may not have owned their own business, but the people at NASA thought like entrepreneurs. As challenges mounted and Apollo 13 appeared destined for disaster, the engineers and astronauts in crisis pulled together and kept their priorities straight, demonstrating both vision and single-minded focus. They did not allow themselves or their teammates to entertain failure as an option. Though they each had their own fears that their plans wouldn't work, they didn't dwell on them. They also did not waste one minute pointing the finger at *who* was to blame for what happened. Instead, they got even more creative in their thinking and more receptive to ideas, no matter how crazy these may have sounded at first. They kept their attention steady and unwavering on their goal—and did whatever they had to do to get those astronauts home.

This is how you want to be in your business. Let pressure and high stakes bring your goals and intentions into clear focus. Pull together the right people and resources you need to make it happen. Always stay open to the possibility that you can achieve more than you think, even if you're not sure how you will do it. Do not give in to fears, self-doubt, or urges to give up. And don't get stuck blaming others or wallowing too long in indecision.

Running a company can challenge your perseverance and resolve, because there is always the possibility that you will not be as successful as you would like, or that you may out-and-out have to walk away. And yet, your outcome is not left up to chance. If you set out to do something extraordinary, and then pull together a team of special individuals and put all your talents to work, you can make what seemed impossible possible. And that pays off in both financial rewards and fulfillment. It is a mind game. That is exactly what makes being an entrepreneur so exciting.

Entrepreneurial Mind Traps

In all the years I have worked with businesses and individuals to maximize their companies' profits and performance, I have found at least four ways that people tend to stand in their own way. I call them the Top Four Entrepreneurial Mind Traps, because they can hold your entrepreneurial spirit hostage and kill any chance of fulfilling your dreams. They are insidious because we often don't even realize that these negative tendencies are present in our thought processes. The only way you can recognize one of these limitations is by examining your results. If you aren't getting the results you want, one of these traps may be sabotaging your success.

Pay Attention to the Right Things

Throughout this first section of the book, we focus on all the internal mechanisms that do not work well for you and your company, so you can then replace them with effective habits that establish patterns of success. Positive results come from *redirected focus*. In the coming chapters, you will learn some specific processes for dismantling these Mind Traps.

Top 4 Entrepreneurial Mind Traps

Misplaced Focus→	Negative Result	Redirected Focus→	Positive Result
#1: Fear (focus on future)→	Paralysis	Focus on present→	Passion
#2: Complacency→	Pain	Engagement→	Positive Expectation
#3: Blame→	Powerlessness/ Problems	Focus on Responsibility→	Possibilities
#4: Indecision→	Procrastination	Action→	Progress

The Wrong Stuff

Here is how each of these entrepreneurial mind traps can hurt your business. As I give you this "what if" scenario, think about how each one may be holding you back. Make a note of them, because we will remedy them all.

Imagine if the crew at NASA had allowed their focus to stray to the wrong things. Making negative predictions based on their worst **fear** would have sent them into **paralysis**: "*They'll never make it! Statistically speaking, it's impossible.*" These are the fearmongers at too many companies, who waste their time and talent contemplating worst-case scenarios just so they can appear wise when it comes true. Then they say, "See? I told you that would happen."

Fear blinds the mind's capacity to see all available options and possibilities. That's why those who are run by anxiety tend to run around in a directionless frenzy and make little progress. Without options, they feel hopeless. Hopelessness leads to apathy ("Whatever . . .") passivity ("I can't do anything anyway . . ."), and complacency ("I'll just go along with what everyone else is doing, so they can take the blame when it all goes wrong.")

Complacency is *not* easy to recognize, because it is the norm. We're so used to hearing those who cannot imagine possibilities stand around the coffee machine commiserating about their *pain* that we don't bother arguing with their false logic. Then we disguise our helplessness with *blame*, complaining about everything and everyone else for making us miserable. There is always an easy target, a great force at work that we can point to. But what does that get us? We feel powerless and desperate. Worse yet, when we totally strip ourselves of any responsibility we also strip ourselves of the chance to change things.

This sense of powerlessness then makes us feel stuck in *indecision*, so we *procrastinate* because we've stopped trusting our ability to make anything happen. That is how easily we can fall back into the model of mediocrity. We fall asleep at the wheel and lose control over our lives.

If the NASA crew had procrastinated in indecision, they would have just let the clock run out on those astronauts. They would not have been emotionally engaged in a positive outcome. As soon as five o'clock rolled around, they would all go home saying, "Those guys are all going to die. It's your fault, and anyway, there's nothing we can do about it now."

That may sound like an impossibly ridiculous scenario—unless you have ever experienced corporate culture. Then you know firsthand how fear, complacency, blame, and indecision are negative states that inevitably get bad results.

Entrepreneurial Trap #1: FEAR

Misplaced Focus →	Negative Result	**Redirected Focus →**	Positive Result
#1: Fear (focus on future) →	Paralysis	Focus on Present →	Passion

Fear is always a result of focusing on a negative future—dwelling on what you don't want. The remedy, then, is to focus instead on the present and your power of choice. How many people in today's world are sitting back saying, "I don't like my life, but I'm afraid to make a decision to change anything"? They fear new beginnings with no guarantees. In their attempts to avoid change, they get stuck. Worse, they can't see the opportunities all around them.

This is how fear robs us all, as individuals and as an economy. Out of fear, the start-up never calls that capital investor, the entrepreneur never makes his business needs known, and the entrepreneur never makes that all-important next move that could triple her market share. But the *biggest* risk is that you let fear stop you in your tracks, so you never fulfill your deeper longings.

It is not fear itself, but how you respond to fear,
that determines your level of success and fulfillment.

Passion Returns

Fear can also be a great motivator—at first. The mere thought of failure, loss, humiliation, pain, or death—real or financial—can provide just the type of stress that translates into action. A deadline, for example, can create the kind of panic that motivates us to stay focused and get a job done. The anxiety and the adrenaline that pulses through our body speaking in front of a big crowd can get us to perform our best. And the fear of losing our shirt when we start a new business can force us to learn fast.

Ideally, fear stays with us just long enough to give us a glimpse into what really matters, what we truly want to do with our time, what we wish we had acted on when we had the chance. At that point, to enable us to correct our course and carry out our new vision, passion must replace fear.

Got Fear? Get Present.

The problem with fear is that it can prevent you from taking action that could advance your position. When I was twenty-seven, I went to live in a small town in Japan, to learn martial arts from a grand master, a traditional Japanese sensei with a direct lineage in a Samurai bloodline. I had no fear of traveling on my own, being one of the only non-Japanese students there, or subjecting myself to the rigorous discipline required. It turned out, however, that I did have a phobic response to being choked. I compensated by getting really good at avoiding choke holds. Still, no matter how good I got at other skills, I could not progress to the next level. At some point, the grand master figured out my weak spot.

One morning as I walked in, he looked at me and said in his broken English, "We work on chokes today. Get on your stomach."

I lay down on my stomach, and the biggest guy he could find positioned himself on my back. Instantly, my heart rate jumped to well above 160 bpm. I was in panic mode. My vision blurred, my breathing got shorter and shallower, I lost the use of my fine motor skills, and I couldn't think straight enough to know how to defend myself. My options and abilities were very quickly diminished. Seconds later, I got choked out and blacked out. My worst fear came true.

Sensei woke me up and said, "Do it again."

I blacked out a second and a third time before I could even think. I was fighting so hard to avoid that choke hold that I wore myself down.

When Sensei brought me some water and said "do it again" for the fourth time, I took a deep breath and said to myself, "Okay, this strategy is not working. I need to find some way to move beyond this."

This time, I took a deep breath and got very present with my fear, my heart rate, and then moved my attention to my breathing, as we had been taught. This time, I stayed focused long enough to break free of my ingrained response and into another level of performance. My teacher had given me the opportunity that I didn't want to give myself: to face my fear in that moment and transform it.

Fear is like a self-administered, psychological chokehold. When you let it go, your passion rushes in to take its place. Replace fear with passion—find a goal that is deeply meaningful to you. Here is a great example of what I mean.

Standing on the Edge of a Clif

Fascinated by the tremendous success of Clif Bar, I spoke with its fearless leader. As it turned out, Gary Erickson was not without his fears, yet his extensive experience in outdoor adventuring had taught him how to feel his way through and around fear. As a result, the company continues its epic climb to the top of the health bar industry, perhaps not *in spite of* fear but *because* of it.

In the snack food business, Clif Bar stands tall as a David among such Goliaths as Kraft, Nestle, and General Mills. Because Clif was one of the only privately owned companies in the health bar industry, the day came when Quaker Oats, one of the giants in the snack industry, approached Erickson and his partner with a $120 million offer to buy out Clif Bar. At the point of signing a deal that would put $60 million each in his and his partner's pockets, Erickson found himself paying closer attention to what really mattered to him personally. When the moment to sign came, he decided to walk away from the deal. To do so, he agreed to buy out his partner. So instead of walking away with $60 million in his pocket, he ended up $65 million in debt, at a time when his competition was steep. The sheer magnitude of his debt could have overwhelmed him with fear. But he stayed focused on his ideals: a healthy brand and lifestyle. And Erickson eventually went on to take the company to even greater heights.

I wondered, how did he withstand the pressure to sell out? How had he dealt with the risk of collapsing under the debt he took on so that his partner could get what he wanted, too? Here was Erickson's response:

> *I don't feel like I'm a super hard-core world champion or anything, but I've had enough experience rock climbing, mountain climbing, and biking, as well as traveling to countries where I've faced a lot of unknowns. I've gone through tough times, injuries, the ups and downs of bike racing. I've been through risk. This didn't feel that different. There was a lot of money at stake, sure, but the essence of it didn't feel any different than all those other experiences. Whether it was climbing Half Dome or traveling to India, it was just another risk.*
>
> *Clif Bar came out of a passion. It was a passion for food, but it was also passion for cycling, so whether it's one thing or a combination of things, people have to be kind of in love with something or passionate about something and really absolutely believe in it. Once you're going, never give up . . . Life needs to be lived now. Not at the finish line. It's not about getting rich. The healthy lifestyle is what it's all about. The profit just supports that.*

Erickson's singular passion continues to guide his company through every storm. When you are totally focused on your dream in the moment, you exude passion and presence. This is true inner wealth. Profit is built on that.

Transform Paralysis Into Passion

Focus is a double-edged sword: you get what you what you want, or exactly what you *don't* want, depending on where you place your attention. The trick is in turning fear of the future into *excitement* for the future. Passion will propel you further than fear.

Success is a matter of mind over methodology. Move your mind
beyond what you don't want, and on to what you DO want!

Think of your time and attention as if it were money—you can waste it on junk or you can invest it in what is meaningful and valuable to you. The difference is, if you lose money, there are ways to get it back. Time, once spent, can never be recovered. The lesson is to invest your valuable "headspace" in doing what you are passionate about.

Use Your Inner GPS

As a caveat to this, some fear *is* warranted. It's important to listen to what your fear is trying to tell you. Learn to use your inner GPS.

From the age of eighteen to twenty-one, I used to do stunt work for live shows and films. One day, I was standing on top of a four-story building, getting ready to jump, when something inside me told me not to do it. I had just finished three successful test jumps preparing for the actual jump. This last one didn't feel right, but I couldn't pinpoint any reason. So with everyone on set waiting, I ignored the fear. I made a running leap through the candy-glass window and started dropping. Flying through the air, I looked down and noticed that I had passed the target marker. Had it not been for two other stuntmen, who ran over to catch my legs, I would have landed halfway off the airbag and crushed both legs. Instead, my legs came down on them, dislocating one their shoulders. So here's what's good about fear.

I remember my stunt teacher, Rick Meadows, telling me that too many stuntmen get killed because they ignore their intuition. He said, "Fear is the voice of the unconscious mind, which sees and processes in much greater detail than the conscious mind can. It does so without critical judgment. It always has your best interest in mind."

When you're starting a business, a healthy fear may be informing you that you need to develop your strengths in finance or management, or warning you not to hire a certain prospective employee, for a reason you can't detect consciously. Let your unconscious mind inform your conscious choices. This is your inner GPS, which can guide you at all times throughout your career—*if* you keep it turned on.

Now you are headed away from fear and toward fulfillment. Done consistently, this technique transforms whatever fears are holding you back, turning them into passion. This next chapter will help you access that passion by improving your long-range vision.

> To access free training and more resources go to:
> **www.theentrepreneurssolution.com/resources**

CHAPTER 4

CLARITY IS THE CURE

Vision: Define Your Identity, Intentions, and Ideals

The deepest secret is that life is not a process of discovery, but a process of creation. You are not discovering yourself, but creating yourself anew. Seek, therefore, not to find out who you are, seek to determine who you want to be.
—Neal Donald Walsh

CLARITY = Focus + Vision

You may have heard this story before, but I've changed it slightly to show you the importance of asking yourself the right questions.

Once a traveler was walking through a small village in the mountains when he came across three men laying a foundation of bricks. Curious, he asked one of the workers, "What are you doing?"

Without looking up from his work, the man said, "I'm laying bricks. I'm a bricklayer."

"Oh," said the traveler. Not quite satisfied with that answer, he walked a bit farther to where another man was laying bricks.

"What are you doing?" he questioned.

"Building an archway," said the worker, "so I can feed the family."

"Oh, I see," the traveler replied, moving on to the next man.

"What are you doing?" the traveler then asked the third man.

"Building a cathedral!" he exclaimed. "For the whole world to enjoy for centuries to come!"

This story is usually told to motivate employees to have a grander sense of purpose, like the third bricklayer's, when working on company projects. But as entrepreneurs, we are all cathedral builders and bricklayers. To build a top-notch business from the ground up, we need all three perspectives. Like the first bricklayer, we focus on the day-to-day details that set the foundation of our success in place. It may look like grunt work from the outside, but we take pride in it because we identify with what we are creating, so we want to do it well.

In my first job at the accounting firm Peat Marwick, I was like the first bricklayer. I was extremely focused, and I was willing to do what most others at the firm were not. I stayed late many nights with my head buried in books, studying the details of every case, and all the hard work paid off. I got a reputation: *when no one else can figure it out, Mel will get it done.* I was promoted so quickly through the ranks that by the time I was twenty-seven, I was halfway to partner. Though I didn't stay with the firm, I later applied the same work ethic and discipline in my own business. The point is, if you have high standards for yourself, you will live up to the same high standards in your business.

Like the second bricklayer, we are driven to work hard by knowing what is important to us. We want to be profitable so we can take care of the people and priorities that matter most to us. So we design the other three areas of the blueprint: the *marketing*, the *mechanics*, and the *money*—that is, we oversee sales, operations, and financials. And remembering why we do it—whether it's family, health, creativity, sustainability, or just enjoying life—our *ideals* keep us motivated to do better all the time.

The third bricklayer's attention is riveted on the project as a living creation. He remains excited because his higher intention is that his work be culture changing, that it be meaningful to others and serve his community indefinitely. One of your most important jobs as an entrepreneur is to communicate such a clear and compelling vision of the future you intend, with so much infectious enthusiasm, that it compels everyone you need to jump on board. Then your job is to give clear direction to the people on the ground to accomplish it.

It's time to build that vision. Start by laying the foundation: your company's *identity, ideals*, and *intentions*. This is where your mind-set will be the cornerstone of your success.

Building the Vision

Before you ever graduate from college, you will be asked many times, "What do you plan to do with your life?" (meaning, "How do you plan to earn money?"). Once you get a job, you will be asked hundreds more times, "What do you do?" (meaning, "How do you earn money?"). But you could go your whole life without ever being asked, "*Who* are you? *What* do you really want? *Why* is it important to you?"

I promise you, this is not just a philosophical exercise. The three "I's" are all crucial to the building of empires. Everything in the human-made world exists because it began in someone's mind as an idea. Even if you think you don't have a great imagination, the seeds of your business are innate within you right now as your interests, talents, and values.

IDENTITY — Who Are You? And Who Do You Want to Be When You Grow Up?

Ask a child, "What do you want to be when you grow up?" They give you a whole list. They want to be a doctor, an astronaut, a dancer, and a botanist. This is the expansive thinking of a child . . . and an entrepreneur. They start with pure imagination and belief, then keep an open mind to the possibilities.

Whatever we perceive as true about ourselves carries forward into our personal sense of Identity as an adult and an entrepreneur. How you label yourself can determine the parameters of how far you can go.

As a child, Richard Branson was encouraged by his parents and his grandparents to go out and explore the world around him and to take on new challenges even when he was unsure he could figure them out on his own. What a gift to give a child: the chance to have fun and see what you're capable of. It's very different from "do as you're told, and don't make waves." It's no coincidence that Branson creates businesses based first of all on what is exciting to him; *then* he explores their viability. And he doesn't stop at being just one thing: a publisher, a record store, a music label, an airline, a cell phone service provider, a winemaker, or an explorer—the list goes on. He has three hundred different companies and counting.

We all have this same childlike capacity to continue to grow and test out who we are and what we want to be when we grow up. But few of us were conditioned and encouraged to approach our lives as one big, fun experiment.

Identity Crisis

Most parents do not intentionally hurt their children's self-image and stunt their dreams. And yet, I think it's at least naive, if not downright irresponsible, for parents not to realize the powerful effect their words have on young, developing minds. When parents constantly remind their children, "You have limits," *they* are the ones actually limiting them.

Living in a culture that requires flexibility and versatility, we can no longer tell our kids to play it safe and stick with what they know. In this age of new, expansive possibilities, we as parents can no longer suppose that our children need learn only one skill, go down one road, and stick with it. No, they need to develop *multiple* skills and, more importantly, be expansive in their thinking so they can continually gauge which of the many new roads opening up before them to go down next.

And we can have the same type of impact on those we work with, whether employees, vendors, or contractors—so we should be ever mindful of how we interact with them.

When You Lead with Your "But," You Are Going Backward.

For most of us, the challenge when we were younger was that we relied on family for support. But those who love us will often discourage us from doing anything they see as potentially risky. They may have thought it cute when, as a child, you wanted to be everything from a rock star to an ambassador, but at some point, they want to protect us from ourselves. It's very common to believe that life is safer for those who stay within the acceptable norm. Our loved ones may have started with comments like these: *"But let's be realistic, my dear."* Or *"But aren't there already enough experts in computers these days?"* Or *"But, honey, you don't know anything about that. Why not just stick with what you know?"* When you lead with your "but," you are going backward. They didn't *intend* to stunt our potential, but that may have been precisely the effect their good intentions had.

Check the Label

Here's another disservice we do to our employees, our kids, and even ourselves. We give them labels based on their limitations rather than on their best qualities. Thinking this simplifies things, we give them labels: *"He's OCD" "She's ADD."* *"She's an introvert and not very good in social situations." "He's a bad test taker."* Then what do we do? We compensate (and perhaps medicate) instead of educate.

In business, we may judge someone based on their initial performance and then, for the remainder of their tenure working with us, view them through the same tinted lenses. This never allows them to develop fully, because they now have a label that biases our view of them—and possibly their own view of themselves. To allow people to continue to grow and rise to their true potential, it's important not to label them or box them into a confining perception of themselves, because this can create a self-fulfilling prophecy.

Choose Liberating Labels Over Limiting Labels

By giving ourselves convenient but limiting labels, we drive down expectations for ourselves. We give ourselves the perfect excuse to relinquish responsibility for our results. In the same way, someone else, with loads of potential, gets put in an invisible box because some authority figure who "knows more" has defined her or him. Now the labeled person operates as if the box were real.

We do the same disservice to ourselves in business: we focus on what we think are our shortcomings, or we limit ourselves to one or two positive attributes—then we draw conclusions about what we can and cannot achieve: *I wouldn't be a good manager—I'm too nice, or I'm bad at math, so I could never run my own business.*

How do you label yourself? You are living either up or down to your own expectations. Look more closely than you ever have at how your self-perception—the positive and negative aspects of your identity—is shaping both your successes and your constant challenges.

INTENTIONS—What Do You Want?

Your intentions are the goals you hope to accomplish. It has been said that we overestimate what we can accomplish in a year, yet underestimate what we can accomplish in a lifetime. I say:

> *Instead of starting a business that will help you make a reasonable living, start by having an "unreasonable" idea of the life you would love to live.*

As a young son of immigrant parents, Tony Hsieh, of Zappos.com fame and fortune, was on a constant quest to avoid boredom and seek out what was interesting and fun for him to do. While growing up in Northern California, he started a few small mail-order businesses from home and got hooked on the thrill of receiving money in exchange for things he created. After college, he discovered that he was not like most people who just wanted to find a safe, secure job at a company. He still liked the challenge of figuring out clever ways to turn a profit. So when he hit on the idea for Link Exchange with his friend, they quit their lucrative but boring jobs to apply their minds to creating as valuable a service as possible for their users. When it worked so well that he and his partner were offered $1 million for it, they didn't take the buyout. Why would two guys in their twenties turn down such a great offer? They were having too much fun running it. They had created a "tribe," as Hsieh called it—a fun, close family culture that he didn't want to give up. His work was his play.

As soon as the company grew beyond his capacity to personally know everyone who worked for him, he realized that the culture was lost. He wasn't as connected with his team, so it stopped being as fun. He chose to sell it, less for the money than because it wasn't meaningful to him anymore. He sold it to Microsoft for $265 million and even passed on the opportunity to work there for millions more, because it wasn't worth the boredom of doing a job that didn't challenge him. He was uninspired and unmotivated. At this point, he had made the decision to "stop chasing money and start chasing happiness."

Hsieh's financial goal in 2008 was to hit $1 billion in gross merchandise sales by 2010. In his quest for that ever-elusive sense of fulfillment, they far exceeded their goal.

The more precise your goals and intentions, the more likely you will achieve them. Just don't make the mistake that most new entrepreneurs do: start a business solely to answer the question *how can I make money?* Money is actually not a good enough motivator for sustainable success. Instead, consider this question: *What will make me feel fulfilled?* Then let that serve as your motivation.

IDEALS — Why Do You Want It?

Get a Great Idea

If you are still in the stage of your business where you are weighing ideas, make sure the idea is congruent with your ideals—what's important to you. This alignment packs a powerful punch when it comes to creating incentive.

Having vision is more than having long-term goals for your future. It is having a deeper purpose behind the goals and intentions you set, and actions you are taking. *Why* are you doing it?

Your *identity* (self-beliefs) is your powerful vehicle; your *ideals* (core values felt with passion) provide the fuel for the journey. Your *intentions* (specific goals) provide the map and give you the ability to steer through all the twists and turns along the way and hit each point along the journey.

What's important to us may shift throughout our lifetime. As a teenager, you wanted freedom. Around twenty, getting a girl or a guy is important. Later, maybe starting a family grows increasingly more important, and along with that may come incentive for financial security. Beyond those shifting priorities lies a deeper set of core values.

Core Values

Your set of core values is unique to you. They may shift in relative priority, but they rarely change. Ideals are the values that drive you forward. They can also be the emotional states, people, places, and things that are important to you in your life and that motivate you to do what you do. They include the things you can't wait to do as soon as you have a free minute or enough money. Your values should have a big part in shaping what business you choose to do. Core values are your compass throughout your life: they guide which way you go and what roads you take, based on what's important to you. Your list likely includes at least some of these:

- Integrity
- Courage
- Love
- Compassion
- Contribution
- Community
- Fulfillment
- Dedication to Excellence
- Reliability

Knowing your core values will clue you in to the types of businesses you could do well or the culture you want to create. Starting a business you're not passionate about is a recipe for eventual failure—even if it makes money, you pay in lack of fulfillment. Your values become paramount when building a cohesive team. Hire people whose values align with the company's core values but who have exceptional skills for the position. Hint: The more values, talents, and skills you fulfill within your business, the greater the sense of overall fulfillment you will enjoy.

The Entrepreneur's Curse

This comes with a caveat: Don't be so oriented toward lofty ideals that you lose sight of what needs to get done right now to reach those ideals or embody them in the moment. In my consulting practice, I have seen a lot of entrepreneurs suffer from the "entrepreneur's curse": they are so focused on high-concept ideals, they can't focus long enough on the specific tasks at hand to be effective. Or they try to focus on too many projects at once and end up spreading themselves too thin. Their team can't complete any one task before another new great idea is thrown on the table. Or they are so emotionally tied to their vivid ideal picture of tomorrow, they can't enjoy today. This is usually because they are like the third bricklayer: they are so future-oriented and high-minded, with so many lightbulbs going off in their heads, all those flashes of genius blind them to the path right in front of them. And so they stumble over the small stuff—the important details that are right under their feet.

Clarity Is the Cure

If you are too "head-in-the-clouds" and are not making enough progress in your business, get clear about your specific goals and intentions. Break your bigger vision down into smaller and smaller tasks.

> To access free training and more resources go to:
> **www.theentrepreneurssolution.com/resources**

CHAPTER 5

COURAGE

Confidence: Is "Good Enough" Good Enough for You?

You can never cross the ocean unless you have the courage to lose sight of the shore.
—Christopher Columbus

COURAGE = Confidence + Response-ability

During my freshman year in college, I used to work out regularly at the outdoor gym, next to some basketball courts. There was a blind student my age who always walked to class the same way, across the field and past the basketball courts. One day, however, the grounds crew had left a long roll of fencing right in the middle of the field. When the student ran into the roll of fencing while making his usual way toward me with his cane, he began to get frustrated, not understanding the strange new obstacle before him.

Meanwhile, a group of guys shooting hoops on the court all stopped to watch the student slowly move sideways to his right, then almost all the way back to his left. As he struggled to get around this mysterious barrier, the guys on the court started laughing. Finally, the kid got frustrated and sat down. I looked at these guys who were doubled over with laughter, and I looked at the kid sitting on the ground. Then I walked the length of the field and said, "If you hold my elbow, I'll get you to class." As we walked past the ball court, the others yelled out, ridiculing me.

Thirty years later, I still remember everything about that moment. I remember what the guy was wearing; I even remember his cologne. I remember the class I took him to. The only thing I don't remember is his name. That incident had an effect on me. It was the moment I recognized that there are times in life when making a decision may make you unpopular, yet somehow, you still know it's the right thing. This is where you face a choice of values. It takes courage to do what you know is right. And it is up to you to summon that courage. You can choose your own path, or you can choose the one that others lay out for you. You can choose to make a difference in someone else's life, or you can sit back and do nothing.

What does this have to do with starting or running a business? Throughout the course of your newly chosen career, you will face many choices, so you had better find out now what you stand for—and what you *won't* stand for.

Conformity stunts creativity and limits growth potential in individuals and in companies. It takes confidence to tune out criticism and cynicism. It takes courage to step outside the mind-set of seeking false security and fearing financial risk and realize that society's norms are optional.

It takes clarity to make your own path, and it takes courage to walk it. With courage, you are good in a room. You can pitch your ideas and get consensus. With courage, you follow through on your ideas, unswayed by the naysayers. With courage, you are destined for leadership.

The opposite of courage is complacency, the second trap you must avoid if you want to live the life of an outrageously successful business owner.

Entrepreneurial Trap #2: COMPLACENCY

Misplaced Focus →	Negative Result	**Redirected Focus** →	Positive Result
Complacency →	Pain	Courage →	Positive Expectation

Complacency Comes in All Forms

Complacency comes in all shapes and sizes, but it always has consequences. It comes with the belief that we cannot change our circumstances. This leaves us feeling powerless, and powerlessness is stressful. This entrepreneurial trap takes the form of either self-satisfaction or resignation to things as they are: you either don't want things to change, or have the mistaken sense that you can't do anything about the course of your life.

I said earlier that crisis can awaken our senses, clarify our desires, and compel us to take effective action. Living with prolonged stress and struggle, on the other hand, can deteriorate our resolve and dull our senses—or, worse, sap away our drive, so that we let go of the reins of our future altogether. We grow "comfortable" with pain, desensitized to boredom and dissatisfaction. The day begins, and we get to the tasks at hand as if we had received orders and it were simply our job to carry them out unquestioned. This is what seems important in the moment. In this way, our constant discomfort can actually become part of our comfort zone, because it's what we're used to. To the extent that we allow ourselves to go numb, we go nowhere. Fulfillment lies somewhere outside this comfort zone.

1. Settling for Less Than You Want

Complacency can take over when we get inured to the familiar struggle of trying to make ends meet. We shrink our vision to fit our circumstances rather than the other way around: create our life to fit our vision. It's called "settling." We would be happy to settle for "security" at this point. The sudden and substantial loss of jobs, homes, 401(k)'s, investments, value, and trust in our financial system went a long way toward revealing the concept of "security" for what it is: a perception

Whether or not we choose to be entrepreneurs, complacency robs us of the riches that life has to offer, because we scale back. We accept less. And our passivity and lack of drive do not position us to be valuable in any market.

2. The "Everyone's Doing It" Attitude

Complacency makes it convenient for us to cave to the prevailing mind-set, because "everyone's doing it, so it's okay." It's the Wall Street executive who accepts millions in bonuses from mortgage-backed investments that he knowingly misrepresented as "safe."

Pressure to conform dogs us from the kindergarten classroom to the locker room, to the boardroom. Trying to "fit in" is the biggest trap of all for the entrepreneur. It takes courage to go for your dreams. It takes even more courage to stand for something great. Your courage must be greater than greed. Since corporate deception has sacked our economy, we have seen the negative consequences of greed. Greed can move you toward a short-term goal, but it isn't sustainable in the long-term, and it isn't good for everyone involved. Greed has a "winner" and a "loser," but eventually (and not always apparently), even the winner loses.

3. "I'm just doing it the way it's always been done."

Part of the model of mediocrity is to follow what others have done before you, because it seems less risky than thinking for yourself. It's an unquestioning acceptance of things as they are.

I discovered this the day I signed on at Peat Marwick, the accounting firm that hired me right out of college. I was sent to my very first client job and had to go straight to my manager. "I've never done this," I said. "What do I do?"

My boss replied, "Just look at what they did last year, and do it again." I thought, *if every new guy who comes along is doing what the last guy did, how do things ever improve?* Their only criterion seemed to be time: just do it the way we did it last time, because you've got three hours to do it. I was amazed that their criteria didn't include finding a more effective way for the client or for the business. If companies, like some schools, discourage creative thinking, it's no wonder our economic growth rate has plateaued and declined. When you try to maintain the status quo in a world that is changing at an ever-faster rate, your days are numbered. But when companies encourage entrepreneurial thinking within their organization, they can not only keep pace with the current of change but *get ahead* of the curve and innovate.

Courage: The Antidote to Complacency

Courage is innate in you. You had it as a child. You were naturally curious. You wanted to see what you were capable of. You ventured beyond what you knew and what was safe. You didn't question whether you should try to walk; you actually tried it, hundreds of times, and fell on almost every try. Then one day, you walked across the room, and the rest is history. You didn't question your innate ability just because you started out failing more than you succeeded. You were thrilled, and your family probably celebrated with you. Then what did you do? You took it in stride, and you started looking around for the next new adventure.

Will you make mistakes in your business? Yes—guaranteed! As a child learning to stand up and walk, did you fall down a lot? Of course! So get it out of your head that "mistakes" are something to be avoided. And while you're at it, stop thinking it would be embarrassing if your business didn't succeed. Did your loved ones reject you as incompetent or slow witted when you were trying to walk? Well, though you don't remember, they probably just laughed—then helped you get up again. Surround yourself with supportive friends and mentors who will be right there to encourage you if you fall. Rather than let a hard time erode your self-esteem and make you lose all courage, start thinking of mistakes as your feedback mechanism. Approach mistakes with an attitude of "Great! What can I learn here?" This is living a courageous life. *To feel alive, we need to strive.*

Sources of Confidence and Courage

To be yourself in this world is a spectacular accomplishment. The antidote to complacency is courage. It takes courage to be a creative thinker in a corporate environment. But where do you get the confidence to be courageous?

A strong inner knowing makes you persevere in the face of obstacles, because only a healthy and positive self-identity is sustainable. On the other hand, a negative, unhealthy self-identity will manifest as problems in your business. Success may come anyway, but only in the short term. Your inner strength will manifest in the strength of your company later.

1. Be Willing to Fail

After four years at the accounting firm where I began my career, I told the partners I was leaving. I wasn't happy and wanted to do something different. I actually had the chance to go to a smaller firm, where I would have more control.

In my bosses' eyes, I had "partner" written all over me. So they said, "How much are they giving you? We'll double the increase."

I told them I'd think about it over the weekend.

When I got home, I realized the question was not what I could do with all that money, but how I wanted to live my life. The hours, the nasty politics, living life on someone else's terms, the unhealthy lifestyle—none of it appealed to me. I was afraid I'd just end up like my bosses, and that seemed a terrible waste. Health was important to me. These people would work from six in the morning until late evening, then go out drinking, and do it again the next day and the next. I wanted to have a bigger impact, not a bigger liver.

I was almost halfway to partner, but I didn't want to wait another four or five years to find out whether someone else was going to decide to cap my success level in the company at a certain point. I figured I should be the one to decide my own destiny, and if I should screw up on my own at this stage, I was still young enough to fix it.

I came back on Monday, thanked them for the offer, and gave my notice. I went out on my own and never looked back.

Being an entrepreneur is about living life on your own terms. If I did only what society expected of me, it would never be good enough for me. I was not prepared to die having lived a life of complacency. Is being part of the pack good enough for you?

Courage is willingness to break away from the pack, not just for the sake of being different, but to improve conditions in some way for yourself or others. Confidence comes from your self-worth. Rather than seek validation from others, start to validate yourself. Stop thinking about what you lack, and start to see that you can rely on the skills and talents you do have.

Be willing to fall in order to have it all.

2. Rise to the Occasion

The sources of courage and confidence can be a balance of internal and external factors. Inner validation—believing in yourself and your dreams—is both achievable and sustainable. External motivations such as luxury, fame, and approval from others can produce success, but they are not as fulfilling. Interestingly, it was my ego that gave me the courage to pursue my next challenge.

When I left my second accounting job to start my own firm, I had no plan, but I did have plenty of ego. After years of building my business, I decided to focus on strategic consulting, litigation, and valuation as my specialty. I was looking for more personal and professional growth, along with higher financial rewards, and I saw the opportunity for more challenge. One day, I read an article in the *Journal of Accountancy* about a guy who did valuation, and I called him up. I said, "I want to build a career in this. Can you help me?"

His response to me was, "Look, if you're not doing it now or working for someone who's doing it now, give it up. You can't make it."

I said, "Okay, thanks," and hung up. What he doesn't know is that we speak on the same platforms now.

I had sought him out as a mentor, but he didn't want to be one. Well, he may not have guided me, but he did fuel me—his response elicited a steely desire in me to prove him wrong. Like the space shuttle that uses 90 percent of its fuel taking off, I took off in this new direction. Once I began to enjoy the satisfaction of learning a new specialty and gaining mastery in my field, that was fulfillment enough. I didn't set out to be the top in the industry, but that's where I ended up.

3. Inventory Your Strengths

Acknowledge your wins, no matter how small. If you are going to inventory everything you think you do "wrong," then at least balance that out by asking yourself:

- *What did I do right or well in this situation?*
- *What's good about this?*
- *What do I have to be grateful for?*
- *What are some of my greatest attributes?*

4. Drop the Need for Perfection—Perfection Is for Unicorns

I have seen too many young stars work really hard and develop wonderful skills only to find that in the moment of truth, when they are called to action, they don't execute. It is not because they can't. It's because they are unwilling to appear less than perfect. Here's a story about a young man I trained at the karate school, who did everything right and whose desperate need to be perfect ultimately compromised his performance. I wonder how many people out there go through something like this every day of their working lives.

I worked with a boy for several years as he methodically worked his way up to preparing for his black belt. He was good at it, yet he berated himself constantly. At one of our training sessions, I asked him to tell me ten things he was great at. He had a difficult time doing it, yet it was easy for him to tell me ten things he was *not* good at. I upped it to twenty-five things and made it his homework assignment. An adult student who was standing close by, also a black belt candidate, overheard me talking to the boy and wanted to try listing twenty-five things that made him great. He couldn't do it, either. Here were these guys who, on the outside, had it all together. Most of what they each listed consisted of specific skills such as "I can jump really high." Only a few were actual character traits, such as patience or persistence.

I still had to remind them several times, "We're not talking about what you can do, but what you are." When they still didn't get the distinction, I said, "Okay, you can jump high right now. How about when you're eighty? See?

Jumping is achievable but not sustainable. But when you say, 'I support others well,' *that's* sustainable—you will still be that at eighty." They got it.

5. Tap into Inner Validation

When I lost some of my motor coordination and ability to speak after my accident, I lost what I considered some of my better strengths: athleticism and speaking. But these physical limitations helped me tap into the heart and wisdom that were unique to me.

Whenever you seek validation from others, you don't have dominion over our own self-worth. When you find what is unique to you—and value it—confidence is automatic because you are valuing yourself. Your winning attitude will gain you wins with others, too. Your stronger sense of self will also convince potential partners, employees, investors, and customers of your value.

> To access free training and more resources go to:
> **www.theentrepreneurssolution.com/resources**

CHAPTER 6

RESPONSIBILITY: MISTAKES, DISADVANTAGES, AND OTHER GREAT OPPORTUNITIES

A lot of people are worried about making mistakes, but if you're not making mistakes, then you're not taking enough risks. Taking risks and making mistakes is how you grow, on both a business level and a personal level.
—Tony Hsieh

COURAGE = Confidence + Response-ability

O f course, you want to avoid mistakes and failures when you can, but you can't avoid them 100 percent of the time. So you need to have a tool that will turn those screw-ups around to your advantage. Responsibility is just such a tool. It is the ultimate multipurpose tool that can undo any bad situation you've gotten yourself into.

The word "responsibility" has unwarranted negative connotations. It rings of too much duty and obligation weighing on someone's shoulders, or of taking the blame for something whether you did it or not. It's actually much simpler: *responsibility is your ability to respond.*

Choose Your Responses Well

Although we may not control our circumstances, we can control our responses. Here are the choices: we can get a false sense of power by blaming others for "what went wrong" in our lives, *or* we can gain even more power by assuming responsibility for our own choices. The former is more of a reaction than a response. Reacting emotionally to a person or situation robs us of power and weakens our credibility—not a good way to go if we want to lead. The latter response—assuming our responsibility in any given situation—gives us the mantle of power to change it, while earning us respect.

To show you the power you possess, I'll share a story that I didn't want anyone to know about at first, because it was too embarrassing. But it's such a great demonstration of what I mean by "taking responsibility," I will swallow my pride and share it. Here is a tale in which one situation produced three different responses in three different participants, who then got three very different results.

Before the recent economic bubble burst, the investment market was still attracting investors the way California once attracted gold prospectors. Through a friend, I got introduced to a gentleman with an illustrious career as a hedge fund trader. He was certainly a likable guy, a family man with a wife and four kids. I entrusted a very large chunk of cash to invest in a business opportunity he was managing. The friend who introduced us had been invested with him for more than a year, and then I actually got one of my closest friends involved in the investment, also. Long story short, it turned out to be a Ponzi scheme, and it wiped out a third of my net worth. My friends lost big, too. Between the three of us, we had been taken for over $4.5 million. Millions of dollars swept off the table like poker chips in a game, though it didn't seem much like a game at the time. I was furious and embarrassed. I had gotten Ponzied. Wait a minute—I'm the guy they hire to put these guys away! How did I miss it? I was walking around in a fog of disbelief and what seemed like helplessness. Once I let my own ego get out of my way, I realized that I hadn't missed it—I had *ignored* it.

I had chosen to ignore it because the rate of return sounded so good. It took me a while, but I quickly realized that I needed to do a few things. First, I needed to give my son, Jeremy, the certainty that things would be okay and that I would be able to rebuild. Second, I wanted to make sure Jeremy understood how I had allowed this to happen to me. Only by doing this could I turn the loss into a positive and worthwhile experience—or, at least, a tolerable one.

Mistakes as Life Lessons

Because mistakes are so embarrassing, it's tempting to hide them, to cover them up. I didn't want to teach Jeremy the wrong lessons: *if you make a mistake, blame everyone else so no one thinks you're at fault, or else just shrivel up and die of shame."*

It certainly was a wake-up call for me, and it turned out to be a great lesson, too—in resilience. Though I had ignored my instincts, I survived that stupid decision and was able to rebuild my net worth back, then surpassing it by over 300 percent within four years, using the principles of the Business Mastery Blueprint™. My objective was not just to get the money back, though that was gratifying. To get something good out of a bad situation, I decided I needed to be completely transparent with Jeremy about my bad judgment call. I needed to teach him that mistakes may put you under water for a while, but they don't have to sink you. What sinks you is a crappy attitude.

Meanwhile, my friends handled the same situation in very different ways. One pretty much simply moved on and did nothing. He just adjusted his lifestyle to fit the loss in equity. He was sitting back, as if to say, *oh well. You win some, you lose some* (although he was a little more emotional about it at the time).

He had made some conscious decisions about his life long ago and was intent on living his vision out. He closed his successful business and retired in 1993 after looking at himself in the mirror and asking an intriguing question: "If I were diagnosed with a terminal illness today, would I have any regrets?" He didn't like his answer to that question, so he shut his business three weeks later and retired to live the life he dreamed of. He's now fifty-seven years old—still young enough to work if he chose to. But living his life true to his vision was more important. Certainly, the loss had an impact on him.

Then there was my other friend, who spiraled downward into anger, blame, and self-flagellation. Ultimately, he began destroying his business, his marriage, and his liver through drinking. He has been in and out of rehab a few times since this happened. It took hitting rock bottom for him to wake up and realize that he had better take responsibility for the choices he made, or he would continue slipping downhill. He has recently gone back to school, to reeducate himself for a good profession serving society in emergency situations. This could actually bring meaning back into his life after the long and painful path he had chosen.

Defining ourselves as victims leaves us believing we are helpless to do anything about our circumstances. Many people want to waste time blaming their problems on the government, the president, Wall Street, greedy lenders, brokers, and anyone else they can think of.

Entrepreneurial Trap #3: **BLAME**

Misplaced Focus →	Negative Result	**Redirected Focus →**	Positive Result
Blame →	Powerlessness/ Problems	Response- ability →	Possibilities

Blame is focusing on some else's responsibility, what they did "wrong," rather than on what you can do to make it right. Blame is a good way to go backward or stand still. Assume you are accountable for any results you get. You will free yourself to move forward, and accomplish far more than if you waste precious time and energy pointing the finger.

It's a quick and easy misstep from fear to blame. When you are in the middle of an uncomfortable situation, it's easy to focus on what you believe everyone else did or didn't do to create it. Until you take responsibility for the fact that you are where you are because of your own actions and choices, you cannot get to where you want to go.

Use Adversity to Your Advantage

Shift your thoughts from blame over to personal responsibility. How? By seeking solutions, not excuses. As a business owner, if you are responsible for your success, you should also take responsibility for your failures. When Donald Trump lost all his wealth by overleveraging in the real estate market in the eighties, he said, "I took my eye off the ball." Then he proceeded to make it all back, plus billions more, because he focused on the lessons he could get from his choices, so he could do things differently. He never lost sight of his vivid vision of his future.

Activate Your Ability to Respond

1. Solve Problems Before They Happen

Okay, granted, some pretty bad things have gone down. But you have to admit, catastrophes of Titanic proportions are pretty rare. Often what makes entrepreneurs freeze up at the helm is imagining worst-case scenarios. If you find yourself unable to take action in your business because you are worried about its unforeseen consequences, ask yourself, *what's the worst that could happen?*

Face whatever is worrying you. This is called preparation. Any lack of confidence you are feeling is likely coming from worst-case-scenario thinking (without looking at the possible remedies and alternatives)—and the likelihood of these happening is slim to none. Still, such thinking gives you a chance to see whether your worst fear is warranted, because it will make you prepare for the worst and plan for the best. It's important to ask yourself and your team straight out, *what's the worse that could happen if we botch this job?* It forces you to throw out all your worries on the table and problem-solve before you ever have to face the problem. By looking at all that could go wrong, you gain enough insight and control to come up with all the possible solutions, too.

2. Track and Celebrate Accomplishments

Reflect on where you were a year ago. Or a decade ago. Acknowledge and maybe even keep a log of everything you had to do—and did!—to get where you are now. Consider it a "personal brag book." You don't have to show it anyone else. Just use it when you're getting down on yourself, to remind yourself of all your accomplishments. When you see how far you've come, progress continues to get easier.

3. Have Multiple Options

There's a really simple way to avoid the stress of relying on one strategy and then waiting in suspense to see whether that one plan fails. For example, when Jeremy's business was growing and he was seeing more money than he ever had, he was tempted to quit school. He didn't see the benefit of a degree when his experience was giving him real-world, up-to-the-minute education. I told him something of crucial importance: the degree opens doors that experience doesn't. Based on the Corridor Principle (we will go into more detail on this in a later chapter), doors provide endless options. Why would you want to close yourself off from any of them? And then I asked him if he was enjoying the lifestyle he wanted.

He said, "Pretty much . . . almost. There's more stuff I want to do, but I'm getting there."

"Well, I'll tell you what 'getting there' is," I said. "Create a lifestyle that you can live on with half your income. Take the other half and put it away. Invest it in your future. God forbid this downswing lasts a long time or your business is affected or you can't run it at full capacity for whatever reason— you will still be okay for as long as it takes to figure out something else. Compare that to living the way too many people do: on the edge, paycheck to paycheck, without a way to retirement, so no end in sight. And only three to six months' operating capital in the bank before they reach the edge of that cliff. Set yourself some concrete financial landmarks that will make you feel comfortable enough to make tough decisions without the panic factor.

4. Don't Go It Alone

Get support from others. Start looking around for business mentors and coaches, who have already done well in the type of business you would like to create. Build a circle of like-minded people who can serve as a sounding board for your ideas. They don't have to be entrepreneurs, but they should be open-minded and supportive yet have a critical eye. And tap into our website to become part of a community of other start-ups and entrepreneurs at different stages in their companies' growth. Use them to bounce ideas off or to find business collaborators you can work with.

To access free training and more resources go to:

www.theentrepreneurssolution.com/resources

CHAPTER 7

CONVICTION: THE POWER
OF INTERNAL CONGRUENCE

People with character have internalized—embedded in themselves—the
three cornerstones of confidence: accountability, collaboration, and initiative.
When the going gets tough, they are able to rely on those internal supports.
—Rosabeth Moss Kanter

CHARACTER = Conviction + Action

I was originally going to write this chapter on the importance of confidence, but confidence without a moral compass can be a dangerous thing. On the other hand, confidence *with* a moral compass is character. Take the moral compass away from people with power and confidence, and you get a class of Bernie Madoffs, who confidently drive our economy right off the cliff. These are the people who either (a) have lost sight of the repercussions of their actions on others—namely, that they would take many others down with them—or (b) know full well but don't care. Without character, they willingly risk long-term disaster for short-term gain. Take the moral compass away from CEOs, and you've got Enron and others thinking they are above the rules of the game. Confidence is overrated, while character is so far *under*rated that it seems almost old-fashioned.

Watch the classic 1946 Christmas film *It's a Wonderful Life*, and you recognize that Jimmy Stewart's character, George Bailey, has character. Nelson Mandela's "enemies" put him behind bars for twenty-seven years. And yet, instead of being disillusioned and bitter, he deepened his commitment to peace and justice. He used the time to study and learn the discipline of nonviolence, and when he got out, he led his country in putting his deepest convictions into policy and practice. Instead of exacting revenge, he sought to unite all South Africans.

So what is character? A kind of resilience of values? Humility? Accountability to others? Yes, all that and more. The name Atticus Finch is almost synonymous with character. The lawyer and father in *To Kill a Mockingbird* defends a very vulnerable man who is about to be raked over the coals by an angry mob. He does it for the sake of level-headed integrity and at the risk of his own good standing in the community.

In chapters 2 and 3, you focused on finding your North Star. You got clearer on what is important to you and on some of the core values that you stand for. Now the question is, how are you going to show up? Not just on paper, but in your words and actions.

How Do You Show Up?

What you *stand for* is in your heart and mind. How you show up is in your feet. In people with character, you can't separate the two. These are people who walk their talk.

My father has always exemplified character for me. When I was a teenager playing high school football, he opened our home to the players on the team who were being bussed in from out of town. He didn't want them to have an unfair disadvantage from losing sleep commuting back and forth to school each day. Despite the fact that our already large family was living on his engineer's wages, several of my teammates routinely stayed in our guest room and ate dinner and breakfast with us every day. This wasn't the first time he demonstrated his belief that everyone should have the same chance to make it in this world.

When my father was eighty-one, eight months after my bike accident, he got very ill and had to stay in a rehabilitation center. Knowing how long the hours spent alone were, I went to sit with him in the garden for hours each day. He looked so frail, I found myself having the same thought my son had texted when I was in the ambulance after my accident: *if this is the end, I only hope my dad knows how much I love him.* I thought of some of the people my father had helped in his lifetime. I thought, *I really hope he knows how many people appreciate him for all the support he gave.* Countless strangers are probably grateful to him to this day for heroic acts he performed when he was only a teenager. I hoped he could see that his was a life well lived. So I asked him, "Dad, do you remember how you got out of Baghdad?"

He nodded, "Of course!" and told me the story I had heard only once, from my mother.

He was born in Baghdad during a time when Jews were being beaten and hanged in town squares for practicing their beliefs. As soon as he turned seventeen in 1946, my father joined the Haganah—Hebrew for "the defense." They were only a small group of Jewish immigrants, but they made it their job to guard the Jewish communities against attacks. He and four of his closest friends, who were called the Five Mavericks, began smuggling guns from across the border into Baghdad so that the Jewish sector could protect themselves. Then, when the violence intensified, he and his buddies started smuggling Jews out of Baghdad and across the border. Many of them found their way to a safe haven in Israel or the United States.

Then one day, two of the Five Mavericks got caught. The news spread that his friends were being tortured and giving up names. My father had to arrange fake papers quickly and change his name to Abraham, his grandfather's name. Then, rather than renounce his friends for betraying him, my father and the other two Mavericks sneaked into the house where their friends were being held, and broke them out. Knowing they must now escape Baghdad immediately or be killed, four of the Mavericks fled to Israel. At eighteen, my father slipped over the Iraq border and found his way to America. The opportunity to have an education and a life free of persecution drew him into the great unknown.

As he finished telling me the story, the garden seemed to grow even quieter. I asked him, "Why did you do it, Dad? Why would you risk your life for these people you didn't even know?"

As if it were obvious, he replied, "It was the right thing to do."

My father passed away four days later. Having consistently turned his convictions into actions, he showed me what it means to live a successful and courageous life.

Practice Your Beliefs

Success lies in the courage to act. The imprint of character is in the steps you take. An entrepreneur's character is revealed in his or her company's culture, products, and policies.

In the book *Confidence,* Harvard Professor Rosabeth Moss Kanter defines "character" in those who "internalized the cornerstones of confidence: accountability, collaboration, and initiative." When these traits are lined up and pointed in the same direction, it's called "internal congruence": everything you do is in harmony with your core values. And it is the strongest base to build a company on.

It is no coincidence that Zappos is known for the genuine connections it makes with its customers, vendors, and employees. That's not just policy. Founder Tony Hsieh realized how important personal connections were to him. He put that awareness into practice in every area of his life, and everything changed. The company's "customer loyalty team" dropped their scripts and focused on being real. They handled issues creatively, one on one, without passing the caller off to someone else. They would stay on the phone with the customer for hours if need be. And the word spread. Personal connections led to word of mouth, which then boosted sales and caused Zappos to exceed its profit projections. Hsieh's company culture was consistent with his character.

Living Out of Alignment

On the other hand, when an entrepreneur or any other leader within a company espouses one set of values but demonstrates another in action, this misalignment often leads to an atmosphere of confusion, tension, and unnecessary complications. Just as misaligned tires will cause a car to shudder, a company can careen out of control, brought down by its leaders' state of internal incongruence.

I use these examples to make a point: we all have an innate need to be consistent with our ideals and identity. We feel good when there is continuity in our beliefs and our behaviors. We feel bad when there is a disconnection there. When our picture of ourselves *(identity)* no longer matches up with our best intentions and our ideals *(values)* the mind is under stress. When this state is prolonged, the result is misery, ill health, career-crash-and-burn syndrome, and perhaps even eventual suicide.

Pressure to Conform

Unfortunately, in a culture that conveys a lot of mixed messages, knowing what you stand for is not always that straightforward. We want our kids to "do the right thing," for example, but then, to prime them for the real world, we encourage them to "do whatever it takes." We stress the importance of getting high test scores, yet allow them little time and attention to develop the kinds of creative problem-solving abilities they will need in the "real world," because those skills are too hard to quantify and grade. We tell our children to participate in clubs and sports—not necessarily for their enjoyment or skill building, but to build their résumé. They are so busy doing what is expected of them, they can't follow their own natural curiosity. In other words, we are more concerned with how our kids look on paper than with where their real interests and talents lie. All this sends a message that it's more important to live up to others' standards than to follow their own heart. This leads to lack of fulfillment later as they find themselves not at all sure what matters to them personally.

Intentional Congruence

Working within a set of core principles translates into balance and integrity in your businesses. High Point University President Nido Qubein describes this as "intentional congruence." When you determine what values lie at the core of your being, they become an awesome source of motivation bubbling up beneath your life and business. Your previously fractured life is now unified by purpose, which gives you great range and latitude in your career choices.

Qubein's core principles are the common denominator in all his career choices. He moved easily between several roles: as CEO of Great Harvest Bread Company, magazine publisher, public relations expert, consultant and mentor, and university president. In his book *Life Balance the Sufi Way*, cowritten with Azim Jamal, Qubein describes intentional congruence this way:

> *The principles we live by determine our character—the essence of who we are. When you choose an external source of core motivation, you place yourself at the mercy of mood swings, inconsistent behavior and uncontrollable changes of fortune. When you put principles at the center of your life, you have a solid, unwavering foundation for decision-making.*
>
> *When we live by our principles, we are being true to ourselves. This is quite different from being self-centered. Self-centered people don't reach out to others, and don't concern themselves with others' interests. They therefore live their lives in emotional isolation, often developing mental-health problems.*
>
> *By centering your life on valid principles, you create a stable, solid foundation for the development of your life-support factors. You embrace and encompass the truly important areas of your life. Successful relationships, achievement and financial security will radiate from the principles at your core . . . When your inside and outside worlds are in harmony, you are enjoying intentional congruence.*

The choice I made in 1988 to leave the accounting firm even though I was on my way to making partner was the best decision I ever made. Though I was being offered a pretty healthy raise at the time, I wanted to have a much greater impact on the clients I served, and greater control of my own destiny. After a planned sabbatical studying martial arts in Japan, in 1989 I joined a smaller firm where I could have the professional freedom I wanted. By 1994, I was managing partner. But by 1997, tensions were building between the other partners and me over a conflict of values that came to a head over my booking a speaking engagement in Arkansas.

I remember one my partners looking at me in disbelief and saying, "You're a freakin' accountant from California going to speak at a tax conference in Arkansas? We're never going to get business from there!"

I said, "I don't see that as an obstacle. There are three hundred fifty people in that audience. They don't do what I do. And they *need* what I do."

Their response was, "We're not spending the money to send you. If you go, we no longer want to be partners."

Right there, in that moment, I was presented with my options: go to Arkansas and possibly lose my job; or don't go, and stay at the firm on my partners' terms, feeling penned in by their confining definition of success. Call it stubbornness or call it congruence, my deeper knowledge of what I wanted kicked in, and I just knew that I couldn't *not* do it.

I said, "Okay. If you choose not to pay for it, I'll pay for it myself. But I am going to go." And just like that, I was on my way.

But on the flight to Arkansas, my "other voice" kicked in. I was sitting there asking myself, *what have I done? I honestly don't know if I'm going to make it.* There was so much riding on it. I had just bought a brand-new house that same year . . . I was in the midst of a custody battle for my son . . . I was dealing with three herniated disks in my back and coming off disability . . . and now I was in the midst of a partnership breakup! My life looked a lot like a disaster. I had to remind myself often that where my partners could see only loss—of income, time, and status—I saw a huge opportunity. I kept my attention on my conviction.

When I got to the conference center in Arkansas, the woman introducing me, who had seen me speak before, said, "Y'all buckle your seat belts, now, because this guy goes fast."

I went off like fireworks for two hours. And by the time my plane landed in Los Angeles, I had landed a twenty-thousand-dollar project. Not only had my decision covered my expenses many times over, but I thought, *here's my start-up money for my own firm. As long as I give it everything I've got, the worst that can happen is that I fail and have to go back to working for another firm again.*

My decision was made easier by my overriding need to stay congruent with my values: health and happiness. Had my main objective been to stay in my comfort zone, I never would have grown so tremendously as a person and as a professional. And I wouldn't have gained the experience and inspiration to write this book right now. I would still be working from 8:30 to 8:30 every day in a suit that no longer fit my values.

Character Building

The enemies of character are complacency and ego. Complacency allows us to stay in jobs that are not in alignment with our ideals and intentions. And the ego gets caught up in its own narrow agenda: *you need more money, more status, more stuff, and make sure everyone likes you, no matter what you have to do to get their approval!* Question the ego's self-appointed authority. It's just afraid of the possible short-term fallout of your having a strong, overriding character that ultimately makes the decisions. Look to your convictions.

Your life happens now. Don't wait on your business to make a difference in other people's lives. Begin to live life on purpose today, not next year or when you retire. Remember, your core values create your thoughts, your thoughts create your vision, your vision creates your focus, your focus creates your actions, your actions create your company, your company creates your impact, and your impact becomes your legacy!

To access free training and more resources go to:
www.theentrepreneurssolution.com/resources

CHAPTER 8

ACTION AND THE PRICE OF INACTION

Men are anxious to improve their circumstances, but are unwilling to improve themselves; they therefore remain bound.
—James Allen

CHARACTER = Conviction + Action

What I see a lot of these days is inaction. People with strong opinions that they do nothing to support, and creative ideas that they sit on for years. People who remain in a limbo state between what they see as the either-or choices of fantasy and financial security. They don't see that by taking their chances and going for their dreams, they could achieve *real* financial security, feel alive again, and have a stimulating effect on the economy to boot.

In our economy, we don't have a money problem; we have a circulation problem. I would venture that most people are choosing to play it safe, holding on to their money and their boring, unsatisfying job. In other words, putting off their life until "things get better"—waiting on external changes rather than creating internal changes. We are allowing our worst fears to determine our decisions, and it's creating exactly what we fear most: lack of choices. Not spending is like a self-imposed starvation diet—it generally leads to a cycle of binge eating and spending later, repeating the cycle of depression and inflation. It's not sustainable.

Many people shy away from making the decisions that could potentially advance their position. They'd rather play it safe and stay where they are.

I notice this mind-set in those I consult for, too: most people look at their actions in terms of potential losses instead of potential gains. Then they wonder why it's hard to get ahead in the game. They're not willing to take risks and be accountable for their actions.

The Decision of Indecision

Indecision is the inability to make a choice and act on it. Indecision can come from fear of making the wrong choice, from overwhelm at having so many choices, or from not having enough information to make the choice. The result is always procrastination. A chronic pattern of procrastination will get you nowhere fast.

One of the negative consequences of procrastinating is loss of options. This is how closet entrepreneurs stay stuck in unsatisfying jobs and how even CEOs fall into paralyzing indecision. This is the last—and perhaps deadliest—entrepreneurial trap that you will learn to break free of.

Entrepreneurial Trap #4: **INDECISION**

Misplaced Focus →	Negative Result	**Redirected Focus** →	Positive Result
Indecision →	Procrastination	Decisive Action →	Progress

The procrastinator is the would-be entrepreneur who talks about his great business ideas for years without acting on any of them. It is the CEO who sees the writing on the wall when everyone else in the industry is moving their factories abroad, but loses profit share because he can't decide on a comparable cost-saving strategy. The procrastinator is the person who for years wants to leave her job, yet stays because she can't decide which of her many fantasy lives she should go for. She doesn't take steps to walk out the door, because she has no steps planned for reaching her goal. Don't get stuck on the indecision merry-go-round, believing your future hangs on one decision. Very few life decisions require that you bet it all on black and hope it comes in. Fear of making a bad decision will stop you in your entrepreneurial tracks. The sooner you face the reality of your current situation, the sooner you can see alternatives. The sooner you act, the sooner you know whether you are going in the right direction.

Indecision often comes from the mistaken idea that *once I make a move, I can never go back. In other words, I don't want to burn any bridges, so I'm not going to cross any.* When we first start a company, we feel that every little decision we make is setting our course in stone, and this makes us reluctant to decide anything at all. We can get stuck because of this wrong thinking. A single decision only sets a plan in motion. It isn't until a series of decisions are made that a direction is set. Even then, you will get feedback along the way and will be able to adjust. You can make the next, more informed decision based on the information you got from the first.

Each decision is simply a dot along the path of growth and learning. Ultimately, your business is a result of a series of dots that create a line or path. Knowing that you have flexibility at all times gives you the confidence to take one action . . . then another . . . and another. This is the basis for the Corridor Principle.

The Corridor Principle

A study conducted at a university over a period of thirteen years found that almost all the people who graduated from there succeeded in a completely different discipline from the one they had originally chosen. But what got them to success was their willingness to *move forward in a direction by taking action steps.* They called this "the Corridor Principle." As entrepreneurs, we start off down one particular corridor, and if that path is somehow blocked, we take a new direction or strategy, down another corridor. Small decisions in the moment create the destination. This illustrates how 90 percent of grads arrived at the area where they found success, even when it differed from their original plans.

Whether you win or lose is not based on one decision; it is determined by countless daily decisions made over the course of your lifetime. A decision is a step. When you line the steps up, they make a path.

Afraid to Make a Bad Decision

Too many would-be entrepreneurs freeze up just because they're afraid they will make a bad decision. Sometimes we stay in bad relationships, unfulfilling careers. We say, "It's a difficult decision." No, it's easy—we are just wrapped in emotions. Or we choose not to leave a job, because we care what others think of us. This is how so many end up living the loss-aversion life, thinking, *if I don't do anything, at least I can't do anything wrong.* Instead of playing to win, they play *not to lose.* That's never an effective strategy in business.

Play to win. Even if a bad decision ends in disaster, it still moves you forward in the game—as long as you learn from it.

When legendary CEO of General Electric Jack Welch was still an unknown manager in a small plastics division within GE, he literally blew the roof off one of their factories while experimenting with a new chemical process. He said, "My confidence was shaken almost as much as the building I destroyed." He went to his manager's office expecting to get berated or even fired. To his surprise, his manager was interested in only one thing: what Welch had learned from the accident. That terrible event taught him how to avoid a much larger-scale mistake in the future. He also learned a great lesson in managing, and he put this belief into practice as a leader: "When people make mistakes . . . the job at this point is to restore self-confidence."

The love of taking chances lures many entrepreneurs to start a business. Turn your fear of the unknown into the *thrill and excitement* of the unknown. It can bring out the best in you.

Okay, now you understand the psychology behind decisiveness and indecision. The question is, how do you get unstuck? Here are several ways. Experiment with them and choose the ones that work best for you, or use them all.

How to Get Unstuck

As Tony Robbins likes to say, *"Your decisions determine your destiny."* Not making a decision is itself a decision. When you're not moving forward, you're falling behind. The question becomes, *if you are procrastinating on deciding your future, who is deciding it for you?*

Options for Overcoming Indecision and Procrastination:

1. Get more information.

You have an idea for a business, but you are waffling, unsure which way to proceed. In most cases, it is simply a case of not having enough information. Cure that lack of clarity by finding the missing information so that you can make a conscious decision rather than allow your indecision to make it for you. Don't get stuck in perpetual information gathering, though, for that is just another excuse *not* to act: *I need tons more information before I can move on this.* Setting your ideas into motion will give you the extra information you need to proceed. The process of running a business is much like flying a plane: you will always be gathering information and using it to make better decisions and course correct. It will be a constant in business if you wish to stay on the growth path and the leading edge.

2. Have clear short-term goals.

Want to know how thousands of hikers have gotten to the top of Mt. Everest? Tiny steps. And perseverance. So turn your lofty long-range dreams into tiny steps. Work backward from your future to where you are today, by asking yourself, *what has to happen before that can ever happen?*

Write down everything that comes to mind until you have worked all the way back to what needs to happen today. That is your small step. It's all you have to do today—no need for overwhelm.

3. Imagine not taking action on your dreams.

Sometimes just the mere thought of not acting gets you to act. Play out your whole life and imagine what you would be like if you never followed your passion.

Regret is a long-term pain. It almost never goes away. The price of inaction is too great. Anticipated disappointment can compel you forward—as long as you don't let yourself get convinced that you have already failed, and give up.

4. Get someone to hold you accountable.

Sometimes, we know the right thing to do, but we're confused by conflicting emotions or other people's agendas. If you are confused because your "rational" mind is telling you to do something but your emotions are pulling you somewhere else, find a wise listening ear to get some perspective. Talk it through. Just hearing yourself will help you reason out a decision.

I once had a client, a brilliant businessman, who asked me to step in and negotiate a real estate deal for him. Of course, he was smart enough to do all kinds of business negotiations himself, but he was also smart enough to realize that he wanted that commercial property so badly, he didn't trust himself to negotiate a good deal for himself—he knew that his ego was so invested in being the owner of that prestigious building, he would agree to almost any terms. He sent me in there to represent logic.

5. Commit and stay flexible.

The idea of committing to a plan and then staying flexible may seem self-contradictory. It isn't. It doesn't mean "stay the course" even when everything tells you it's not working. It means that once you make a decision, commit to it 100 percent . . . then be ready to make new decisions as new information arises. If you say, "This is the way and the only way and that's it," you've put on blinders, hiding your other options from view. There are multiple ways to achieve one outcome. Start by setting up alternative routes to your destination, so you can shift quickly. Make a list of actions you could possibly take.

6. Create new pathways to completion.

If you woke up every day and told yourself you were going to drive to the country, then got on the highway, and when the exit ramp for "the Country" came you didn't take it and instead kept ending up in the city, you would eventually have to ask yourself, *why? Why do I continue to avoid the road I want to go down?* We need to take a closer look at what holds us back in our thinking.

How have we set a course for our thoughts to sabotage our ability to take effective action? The answers lie within the unconscious mind, where habits determine results. We need to uncover our "strategy for staying stuck," so that we can use the same mechanism that got us stuck to get us *un*stuck.

A habit forms as a patterned way that your brain consistently gets you the same result. For example, the moment you decide it's time to brush your teeth, your brain sends all the right signals to the rest of your body to make that happen. While your conscious mind is busy thinking about your schedule tomorrow, your right hand reaches out for the toothbrush as the other hand reaches for the toothpaste. Before you know it, and without thinking about it consciously, you've completed the act of brushing your teeth. It was a complete success.

Your unconscious mind pulls off this sort of successful strategy all day every day. You reach for the doorknob and successfully close and lock the front door. You drive to work and manage to avoid hundreds of cars and curbs on the way, while you sit there planning your weekend. At some point, you didn't know how to do that and had to learn. Once you learned, it became a habit. Now you can create good business habits in the same way. Once you learn new strategies for making decisions or taking action on client calls, they can become as routine as brushing your teeth.

Recognize the moment your procrastination pattern takes over. Notice the thoughts that derailed your intention to pick up the phone or attend a network meeting or update your website. Become aware of the fears or negative assumptions that your mind generates to thwart your best efforts to get a task done.

7. Create emotionally compelling motivation.

Social entrepreneurs tend to be highly motivated to spring into action compelled by their strong convictions about justice and equity.

Indecision and inaction are the unfortunate result of not having clear convictions or clarity of purpose. An emotionally compelling reason is an even better motivator than money for getting the entrepreneurial juices flowing. If you are being indecisive, ask yourself:

- *Why do I want to do this particular business?*
- *What benefits does it bring? To whom?*
- *What is meaningful about it to me?*
- *What would be the positive consequences, the best outcome, if I did it successfully?*

Those positive outcomes are what you are giving up by not making any decision at all. Hopefully, that's a pretty sobering thought for you. That's good, because the best motivation is a compelling future.

Like Atticus Finch in *To Kill a Mockingbird,* inequity alone gives some entrepreneurs the necessary motivation to act. When the future becomes emotionally compelling enough, you will take action without hesitation. Focus on the source of your own motivation until it increases. Rather than wait for you to push yourself, that future will pull you toward it. Ultimately, a strong enough desire, cause, or belief will make your choices clear and compel you to take effective action.

> To access free training and more resources go to:
> **www.theentreprenuerssolution.com/resources**

Connect With Others and Create Community

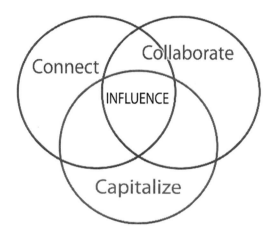

The key to influencing people is to understand them. Part Two gives you a whole quiver of skills that will work for you on several levels—internally in your business and externally in your marketplace—to connect with the people you need: clients, contractors, customers, family, friends, and anyone else who can help move your company forward. It takes a community to build a successful company. This section is about how you reach out to that community. This will come about as a result of your understanding the next three essentials and their respective building blocks: **connecting** (empathy and communication), **collaborating** (partnering and innovation), and **capitalizing** (perception and monetizing).

CHAPTER 9

EMPATHY: THE ART OF KEEPING IT REAL— MEANINGFUL IS MEMORABLE

If you have the right culture, everything falls into place.
—Tony Hsieh

CONNECTION = Empathy + Communication

This is where the stakes get higher. Your dream is no longer harbored internally. You have to move out into the world to make and maintain vital connections with customers, coworkers, venture capitalists—you need to reach out and touch them all. These are the people who will form the basis of your success. The quality of your connections will affect your company in many ways:

1. relationships: their strength and loyalty
2. reputation: word of mouth in your local or global community
3. reach: how far word about your company spreads

4. results: how all those connections support your company, people, profit, and planet

People Are Human, Too

I recently heard a news story that was both heartening and disheartening because of the choices people made.

A man traveling in California on business learned that his grandson was on life support in a Colorado hospital. The two-year-old boy had been thrown across the room by his mother's boyfriend and was now struggling for his life. The doctors didn't think the boy would make it, and the grandfather wanted to see his grandson just one more time. He rushed to the Los Angeles airport two hours early for a Southwest Airlines flight to Denver, but the security lines were so long, he was about to miss his flight. Despite his urgent circumstances, Transportation Security Administration personnel would not speed him through the security check. Ten minutes late for his flight, the grandfather finally ran through the terminal to the gate in his socks, resigned to wait for the next flight.

Instead, he found the pilot standing at the gate, waiting for him. The pilot asked, "Are you Mark? I've been waiting for you. I'm sorry to hear about what is going on. They can't go anywhere without me, and I wasn't going anywhere without you. Now, relax. We'll get you there. And again, I'm sorry."

The man's wife had called Southwest to ask if they could wait for her husband. And the pilot had made a decision—one that could have cost him his job but was in line with his values.

I see a lot of start-ups paying too much attention to the wrong things. They get so obsessed with getting the product just right, or so focused on saving money and time, that they forget how to treat *people*. People and product are the two main pieces of the puzzle that have to fit together perfectly. Your product is your vehicle, but your profit is in the people.

The value you place in your people must be genuine, motivated by something more than money. That Southwest Airlines pilot didn't hold up the plane because he thought it would be good for business. (Indeed, it might be very *bad* for him personally.) He did it because his humanity compelled him to. His action happened to reflect well on his company, but it could just as easily have backfired by angering the passengers who had to wait. The company supported his decision, though, because its values and corporate culture were very human centered.

Your vehicle can change over time. And yet, your people can remain and grow with you over time—as long as you value them. GE started out making lightbulbs; now it develops all sorts of sophisticated technology. 3M began as a sandpaper manufacturer. Amazon was a bookseller. Virgin made records; now it's into mobile phones, air carriers, and space travel. In every case, the company's capacity to develop more products came as a result of the trust it had established in its people (its market). Company and customers grew together. Yes, it *is* a popularity contest, so you want to get them to like you. But you can't manipulate their feelings toward you too much. In this age of reality and transparency, keeping it real is the best policy.

Business in the Age of Connection

As a business owner, you can't treat your employees or your customers as mere cogs in a wheel, as companies did in the industrial age. We have entered the Age of Connection, in which companies can fulfill a much greater purpose and function: to serve people's deeper personal needs and, at the same time, bring global communities together. Business is integral to social and environmental changes, for better or worse. We cannot separate our actions and attitudes from our impact. Every company exists to make a profit *and* a difference.

Knowing this, the question then becomes, do you want to be a positive example? Or serve as a warning and cautionary tale?

After being called about possibly receiving a Lifetime Achievement Award from one of the national certifying bodies from which I hold a designation, I was interviewed before the committee as part of the evaluation process. After an hour of questions about the contributions I had made over the course of my career, the panel members surprised me with their last question: "What would you do for world peace?"

I laughed and said, "Oh, it's a beauty pageant, too?"

A member of the committee said they were just curious. I wasn't expecting this at all, so I responded from my heart.

I said, "Well, I certainly don't profess to have the answer for world peace, but I do know this: if every one of us stopped for a moment and did something nice for someone else every day, for no other reason than because we have the ability and the opportunity—even if it isn't our responsibility—it would go a long way toward solving the problems we have today."

The panel said, "Holy hell, that was the shortest answer, and the *best* answer, we've had so far!"

Why is it that most of us don't take the time simply to connect with other people? What is the butterfly effect of one act of kindness? We can never really know, and it doesn't matter—just do it because it feels good. You'll see the results and get hooked.

The Ripple Effect of Empathy

Start by understanding what's important to others. This requires empathy—the ability to read people and meet them where they are so you can then bring them to where you want them to be. Notice others' responses to you. Watch how your emotions, your moods, your words rub off on others in positive or negative ways in all your interactions. When we treat the customer service guy gruffly, this doesn't create a fun day for him. And when we make a small effort to joke around with him, ask about his day or his town, or let him know we appreciate his time, that moment can change his day, even if just a little bit. Notice how, when you take the time to listen, you can *hear* what is behind what they are telling you. Gradually, you develop empathy—your ability to read and understand where someone is in that moment.

Consider this: YOU *ARE* YOUR BRAND. This is where internal congruence comes into play again. You can spend thousands of marketing hours contriving a clever ad or a slick website, or you can take the time to develop a real relationship and make it mutually beneficial.

Profit Is in the People

Being genuine and generous of spirit can make all the difference in standing out from the competition. Here is a genius approach to business that certainly meant a lot to me. After flying into San Francisco one evening on a speaking tour, I had just settled into my hotel room when my computer promptly crashed. My entire PowerPoint presentation was on my laptop, and I was due onstage at nine the next morning. It seemed my only option was to panic. I called the Apple store in San Mateo just before it closed, and got a kid named Ben on the line, to whom I explained my dire circumstances. Instead of putting me on hold indefinitely, Ben said, "Wow, that's rough. I'll do whatever I have to do to get it done."

Ben then stayed another few hours, until ten p.m., to get the computer repaired and working again for me. This wasn't policy, procedure, or protocol—it was just the right thing to do. I was astounded by his kindness and realness. And apparently, I'm not the only one. When I told someone else this story, she told me of a guy from Apple's Genius Bar who made a house call to fix a computer for a bedridden woman who couldn't bring it into the store. *Really? House calls?* How positively old-fashioned! Now, that is pure genius—you can bet that she won't go back to using a PC anytime soon. Apple's Genius Bar serves up a brilliantly novel approach in which customer service trumps corporate protocol.

Make the Connection

A business is an accumulation of human relations that create synergy around an idea or product. You don't get anywhere without this gathering of people. Your success and fulfillment relies on this network of connections. Gain the support of them all. How do you build the value and viability of your company over time? One connection at a time.

1) Be Present

The business world is not as formal and formulaic as it once was. Business is more transparent and more inclusive—more of a personal reflection of you. While we don't always have to be physically present at the office to compete, we *do* have to be emotionally present. That means present in the now.

When you are present, you are at your most resourceful, flexible, and focused. When you are present, you pay attention to the person in front of you. That makes a good impression. You are decisive, which can save your life or your business.

When I was in Japan working toward my third dan (degree) black belt, I had to take a test. Though we had been working with wooden sticks up until this time, my teacher, Sokei Tanemura, surprised me by drawing a real metal sword from its sheath and told me to kneel down in front of him. I had already been through several rigorous tests that day, so I was tired. When he told me the test was for me to avoid his strike as he attempted to cut off my head, I got very present. In the very next moment, Sokei lifted the sword and sliced down through the air toward my head full force. I rolled out of the way and sat up only to see that he was making a second cut horizontally through the air. Without thinking, I rolled away and averted the sword's great, arcing swing again. Had I let my presence down for a second after the success of avoiding the first cut, I would literally have lost my head.

Presence is the only thing that makes you aware of subtle movements and fine nuances in any interaction. Business meetings can get tense. If you spend your time worrying about failure or concerning yourself with what *will* happen, you are not in the moment. You can't be attentive to others when you are listening to the internal dialogue going on in your head all the time, because you are not thinking about how you can serve the client or customer in front of you. Making a connection is never a waste of time. It's what matters. Focus on whatever you can learn from this moment.

2) Keep It Real

On my way to the board meeting of a company I am a director in, I was about to grab a Starbucks coffee when I noticed a small local coffee shop down the block and across the street. So I jaywalked over to It's a Grind. As I stood there staring up at the selection, the kid behind the counter surprised me by asking my name—and not just to scribble it on the side of a paper cup! He actually used my name throughout our very real conversation. The next time I was on my way to Starbucks, I found myself risking a jaywalking ticket again to talk to that kid. I wondered why and realized that, well, a good cup of coffee is nice, but a good conversation is gratifying. Lots of places make coffee these days, but who makes real connections?

The difference that you make in your business most likely will not lie in your product alone. It will lie in your ability to make—and keep—it real. Cultivate your curiosity. Be more interested in others than in telling them all about yourself and your business. Assume that they have more dimensions than simply what they *do,* and make connections on levels other than work.

3) Connect With Loved Ones

You may or may not get the support you want from your closest friends and family when you first announce that you're going to start your own business. Make a concerted effort to maintain and deepen those vital connections that keep you in balance. At the same time, hold on to your convictions and be careful whom you allow to influence your decisions. Don't give someone else responsibility for your success or failure.

During the years after I started my own business, I lost relationships that were important to me, because I took them for granted. I didn't always admit that I wanted their support, and when they gave me feedback that I didn't like, I devalued it. When I finally expressed my desire to write this book years ago, I didn't feel I got the vote of confidence I had hoped for from my girlfriend at the time. What I didn't realize was that it wasn't her, it was me. I was actually influencing her with my own lack of confidence, lack of focus, and fear of making that career leap. My own firm was thriving, and here I was, proclaiming that I was going to retire at fifty and write a book. Understandably, she, as well as my friends, questioned my sanity, and my procrastination made them wonder whether I would ever pull the trigger. Instead of selling them on my dream, I sold them on my fears.

Don't let those personal connections go because you're "too busy." They enrich your life in ways you may not understand until later. Ask for the support, and when you get it, appreciate it! Businesses can come and go, but loved ones are forever.

4) Connect With Your Team

When entrepreneurs get to the point where they start hiring help, they can mistakenly think, "I'm the boss now. I have to make others do what I want them to do—no more being told what to do." But leadership is not about control and compliance anymore. It's about engaging and enrolling them in a vision, based on mutual respect and appreciation.

It's a mistake to go in thinking that as their leader, you have to boss others around to get respect. Do that, and soon enough, your employees will sit around waiting to be told what to do. That will make more work for you as they stop trusting their initiative and instincts. Worse, you lose all that latent potential for everyone to innovate and work together synergistically. In this scenario, you have created *workers* rather than a *team*. Just because you now wear the CEO's hat doesn't mean you have to maintain a certain "distance" or pretend to be someone you are not.

The Value of Vulnerability

Allow the whole to be greater than the sum of its parts. Profound company cohesion comes out of this. Sustainable success is the holistic way to do life and business, and it's surprisingly simple: let work be fun. The old guard may still believe that vulnerability can and will be used against you. But the reality is, openness and honesty strengthen relationships. Sir Richard Branson is one of the most influential businesspeople on the planet, yet he's just another lad, like the kid on the playground who's always going, "Hey, everybody, let's play this game." He's open, real and attuned to what others want. That doesn't mean he's not a strategic thinker—he's one of the best. But he's also a connector who enjoys engaging others in his wild schemes.

. Business is a team sport. You may be captain of the team, but that just happens to be your skill and your job. Unify the team by bringing the best out in each player.

5) Connect W\ith Your Market

With so much stimulation competing for your market's attention, how do you connect in a uniquely meaningful way with the customers you rely on for your success? Understand where they're coming from and where they want to go.

Nido Qubein came from Lebanon to the United States and wanted to fulfill his potential in a free market, even though he had only fifty dollars in his pocket and didn't yet speak English. How did he connect with his market? He thought about how he could serve his new country. He has done this as chairman of Great Harvest Bread Company, as director of La-Z-Boy and a regional bank, and through other successful enterprises, including as one of the top communicators and consultants in this country, teaching others about how to build financial wealth from their inner resources alone. Then he moved on to his next great challenge: leading High Point University just as he did all his other entrepreneurial ventures: by rendering high value in serving a very specific market. When he arrived in 2006, the university had 375 freshmen. Now it has 1,200 freshmen. Before he arrived, it was number fifteen on *U.S. News and World Report's* list of best schools in the South. Now the university has moved up to number five. SAT scores rose over a 100 points on average, overall enrollment more than doubled, and revenues quadrupled.

How did he make such a radical improvement? More than worldly information, he gave the students real-world skills. In other words, he spoke their language and understood their real needs. Qubein took an organization that is institutional in nature and, in four years, shifted the culture. When I spoke with him, I asked him specifically, "What do entrepreneurs need in order to create that same level of transformation in their businesses?" Here are his words of wisdom and experience :

Entrepreneurs typically possess four qualities. They have a clear vision— they know what they want to do, and they tend to have a keen ability to focus. They have a solid strategy—they know where they are, where they want to go, how they're going to get there. They employ practical systems, not pie in the sky, but almost innately, almost instinctively, they know how to employ practical systems. And, of course, they have consistent execution.

They demonstrate that focused tenacity with a degree of strength and confidence. They act on their ideas. They understand that the results that you get in life are based on the behaviors that you display in life. And the behaviors that you display are almost always fully dependent on the beliefs that you hold dear. So what you believe gets you to act the way you act. The way you act gets you the results that you have.

Entrepreneurs somehow develop the ability to identify an opportunity and then to climb that ladder of opportunity, to sort of light up the pathways for starting something new, feeding it, sustaining it, then benefiting from the rewards that come when it's successful. They tend to have an abundance of energy, and they almost always have relational capital. They know a lot of people, or they know how to get to a lot of people. They know how to build bridges of understanding. They know how to communicate effectively. They can sell their ideas with persuasion.

> To access free training and more resources go to:
> **www.theentrepreneurssolution.com/resources**

CHAPTER 10

COMMUNICATION: THE MECHANICS OF RESOLUTION VERSUS DISSOLUTION

*The greatest challenge to any thinker is stating
the problem in a way that will allow a solution.*
—Bertrand Russell

CONNECTION = Empathy + Communication

Have you ever watched someone trying to get a truck out of the mud or sand and instead digging themselves deeper by gunning it too hard, until they end up *really* stuck? In my experience as an expert witness in numerous partnership dissolution cases, negotiating is the same way. If people come to the table all revved up, talks go around and around, circling the same points; negotiations spin out of control, and no one gets anywhere.

Every Interaction Is a Negotiation

Every conversation is strategic in the sense that everyone involved wants someone else to see their point of view. In some relationships, even how to park the car or clean the dishes can become an ongoing negotiation. Use the Five Rules of Resolution to ensure clear communication and effective negotiations in any situation.

Here's an example: Three partners came to me several years after forming a successful electrical contracting company. The one who ran internal operations and the one who built relationships and brought in contracts believed that the third guy, on the ground overseeing the job sites, didn't shoulder as much responsibility and, therefore, didn't have as much value, so they wanted him out. This crew rushed into the business with a "we'll see" approach. They didn't check whether their ideals and intentions were aligned from the start. They didn't even clearly define each partner's functions or percentage values in their initial contractual agreement. Instead, they triangulated over covert resentments and waited until the company was about to implode before calling me to negotiate a buyout. The problem was, since nothing was in writing, the third partner's "value" amounted to the perception of value. Of course, each partner perceived a different value. I was able to dissipate the tension and resolve the ugly situation, arriving at a value everyone was happy with. I did it using the negotiating skills you will learn in this chapter.

Communication Is Key

Communication in all forms exists for one purpose: to be understood and to understand others. So the first key to making sure this happens is to accept that having yourself understood is 100 percent your responsibility. If the other side doesn't understand what you are saying, then it's up to YOU, not them, to make sure they do. If something doesn't work at first to get your message across, try whatever you think might work. Keep trying. Language is the supremely versatile business tool. Persist, even when it's uncomfortable or frustrating. Don't waste time trying to figure out what others are thinking—ask them!

Don't wait for things to blow over: resolve them before they blow up. Don't wait until after the fact to see if others understood your direction: clarify and get them to repeat back to you what they understand.

Beware of the Land of the Unspoken

There is nothing innately wrong with conflict. Indeed, innovation is often the result of debates brought on by differing opinions. Expect conflict, and use it for your growth.

The rifts between people that threaten the balance of company culture are created in the Land of the Unspoken. This is where lack of communication flourishes and personal rifts fester. What is left unsaid can come back to haunt you and undermine your business and relationships. Catch the smaller fault lines in connections early on, and you prevent larger sinkholes and eruptions that can devastate your business later. Ignoring those "annoying little differences" doesn't keep you in a safe zone—it puts the whole company at risk.

Kinko's President Dan Frederickson had a novel way of ensuring that miscommunications didn't take the company down with them. When a pair of coworkers didn't get along, and before they could divide their departments down political lines of "whose side are you on?" he isolated the pair in a room together until they found a way to resolve their personal issues.

In fact, working out personal differences was so essential to Kinko's staying viable as it grew, the precepts for collaboration were set forth in the company's "Constitution." While most corporations post lofty mission statements in their lobby, Kinko's issued its much grittier "Commitments to Communication." As a how-to guide, it included some impressively subtle distinctions to teach the corporate family *how* to communicate:

- *I will talk with you, not at you.*
- *I will recognize your value at Kinko's.*
- *I will tell you when I don't know the answer, and together we will seek the answer.*
- *I will try to see the situation from all points of view.*

- *I will solicit immediate feedback to ensure we understand each other.*
- *I will not confront you when I am angry.*

That is the level of clarity that you want in order to sustain and grow a family of any size. The guidelines may have been more like hopeful affirmations than actual abilities in some cases, yet they established very clear expectations. The rest was just persistent effort.

The Five Rules of Resolution

Whenever negotiations get positive results, it is because both "sides" used one or more of the following Five Rules of Resolution. I recommend that you adopt this or your own version and issue it to your team for smooth communication:

Rule of Resolution #1: Keep your ego and emotions in check; shift your perceptual position to the other person's point of view.

It's a big mistake to let your ego commandeer the communication process, no matter what the situation. When the ego takes over to assert its narrow agenda all rational strategic decision making and discourse goes out the window. The ego excites negative emotions such as distrust, anxiety, and anger, which can derail progress at any stage. Also, the ego is a ball hog—it will run with an argument in the opposite direction of where you intend to go, just to score its own wins and come out looking good. Don't be fooled into thinking that it has your best interest at heart. When egos take over negotiations, lines are drawn in the sand, and everyone loses sight of the desired outcome.

You know the ego has hijacked the negotiation process when . . .

- it becomes less about finding resolution and more about "not losing" or ending up on top at all costs
- you stay awake all night strategizing all the clever comebacks you can come up with to undermine and undercut your "opponent"
- you try to disguise a petty desire for payback as "a matter of principle"

I was once involved in a custody battle in which a father was trying to gain full custody of his child. He was on track to get exactly that until he decided that he also wanted one more thing: "I want a dollar a month in child support from his mother," he told his attorneys. As with some aspects of most dissolutions, this obviously wasn't about the money. It was about proving a point. Whatever the "point," it is usually not logical and seldom benefits anyone—except the ego. Fortunately, his attorneys didn't have the same emotional investment.

They said, "As women, we will tell you first of all that you just beat up your ex in court. The very next time she has a chance to put your nuts in a noose she will do it, so if you want to go after that one dollar to make it even worse, go right ahead. Second, you'll need to find another firm to do it, because we won't. It's not right."

But how to keep ego and emotions out of it? You may think that dropping your defenses is tantamount to disarming yourself before battle. But actually, there is more power in humility than you might think. The best-kept secret to finding resolution may also be the most challenging: connect with "the enemy." This is known as shifting your perceptual position, so that you can see the situation from another point of view. As a negotiating strategy, seeing from the "other's" point of view opens up vast opportunities for resolution.

The ego is less interested in your success than in stonewalling others. I can promise you, there is no payback in it. In a business context, it is rarely ever a good idea to burn a bridge. Don't lose sight of your bigger goals just for the short-term satisfaction of winning a fight. Keep your connections and friendships. Err on the side of generosity if that's what it takes. See it from the other side. Imagine the other person's experience. And humble yourself enough to express your understanding. You will never regret being generous of spirit.

Rule of Resolution #2: Enter into the other person's world with empathy.

Everyone has a "pain point"—find it and remedy it. What do I mean by that? Here's a great illustration: It was the middle of winter, and I was on my way to a speaking engagement on the East Coast. When I arrived at Chicago's O'Hare Airport, I learned that my connecting flight had been canceled. Suddenly, a mad rush of two hundred upset, inconvenienced passengers was mobbing the customer service counter. Predictably, the airline didn't have seats available. But the crowd wanted what it wanted, and wouldn't relent. Passengers were yelling, chiding, shaming, threatening—pulling out all the most effective negotiating tools for *not* getting their way. As I moved up in line, I heard one guy use the "do you know who I am?" approach, and I thought, I don't want to be *that* guy. How could I flex my communication muscle and respond differently? How could I relate with empathy to the experience of those customer service reps?

I still wanted to get to my destination that day, but I didn't want to contribute to all the discord. By the time I finally got up to the counter, my frame of mind was, *how can I make your world better right now?* She had the power to give or withhold what I wanted, yet I chose not to see her as my adversary, thus bucking the general attitude all around us. Instead, I approached her with an attitude of *hey, you and I are in the same boat.* I asked how she was doing.

Then I said, "Hey, would you like a cup of coffee? I'm going to Starbucks anyway since I've got to wait."

She looked up and took a deep breath. "Thank you," she said. "Yes."

After handing her the coffee, I sat down to wait. My name was called later, and I went back up to the desk. Somehow, she had found a seat on another plane for me, and I made it to my scheduled talk just on time.

The most effective path to influencing others is to understand what is driving them. That's because people make decisions consistent with their needs and values.

Rule of Resolution #3: Stay focused on your ultimate outcome; stay open to the various ways you could get what you want.

What causes most challenges in negotiating is that people get mired in the details. They begin discussions by affirming the points they *disagree* on before they ever look at what they *agree* on. They start stuck, and there's nowhere to go from there.

Start by finding the higher objectives that both sides agree on. Avoid getting caught up in trying to win the smaller battles. It's easier to work from the common objectives down to the details than the other way around.

I consulted with a business owner who was trying to resolve a dispute with her partner. When I asked her what the problem was, she just said, "I don't trust him and he doesn't trust me." As I continued to ask her more specific questions, it became apparent that the root of what appeared to be mutual lack of trust was actually a relatively isolated incident in which there was simply a lack of communication. This was solvable. So I had to ask her, "What do you really want beyond clearing up that one incident?"

She said, "I don't want to have every one of my decisions questioned!"

"Okay," I said, "that's what you *don't* want. What *do* you want?"

"To run the company as was agreed at the outset: I run operations. He is more of a big-picture strategist and financier."

Then and there I got clarity on what she wanted, and it was simply to feel heard and respected. Ultimately, they shared the same goal: they both wanted the company to grow and flourish. However, more questions revealed an underlying difference of goals: it was important for her to build a cool company that she was proud of, whereas he primarily wanted extra cash flow in the short term. The obvious solution was for her to buy him out. So I negotiated that deal, and they both got what they wanted.

Come to the table without prejudice and without labels. Your prejudices establish your expectations. Once you take a perceptual position, it's hard to step back, consider other perspectives, and see your options. Steer a path out of confusion by moving your communication back and forth between concepts and details as needed.

Rule of Resolution #4: Stay engaged and focused on reality; don't let your emotions get the better of you.

Even at the negotiating table, success is more a result of connecting than of competing. If it feels as though you're getting caught up in a competition, remind yourself, that's just the ego setting you up for another fall. And keep your sense of humor! Trying to have it *your* way works only at Burger King. Avoid the pitfalls of focusing on the competition and not staying present. Don't do what I did one night at the Reagan Library and base your decisions and arguments on assumptions.

I went to a charity event at the Ronald Reagan Library, where they were holding a silent auction to raise money for the education foundation in my town. There were several nice items, but when I saw a cardinal red and gold blanket I thought, *perfect!* Jeremy was intending to go to USC, so it would be a cool birthday gift to get him a USC blanket with its school colors for his room. I started the bidding at around twenty bucks. Ten minutes before the bidding closed, I peeked at the card and saw that someone had written in "$50." So I put "$55" and walked away, figuring it was done . . . until I saw an older woman pass me and write in "$60." That did it. I bid $65, so now she was annoyed. She went to seventy-five dollars. So, of course, I wrote in "$85," and she went back in to write "$100." At minute eight and counting, I hit on a clever strategy. I waited until the judge announced last bids; then I walk behind the judge, and just before he grabbed the card, I wrote in "$105." Now I was gloating inside. *I won!*

After dinner and speeches, I went to collect all the stuff I had won, and I tucked the red and gold blanket under my arm. As I was walking out, an older gentleman, probably the woman's husband, came up to me and said, "You're the one who won the blanket."

I said, "Yeah, my son wants to go to USC, so I thought it would be a cool birthday gift."

The man looked a little confused. "I don't know why," he said. "That's a Simi Valley High School blanket."

Simi Valley High was Jeremy's rival school! Not a cool birthday present at all! I walked away laughing at myself. Here I had been so attached to my clever plan that I didn't see reality. I had gotten so caught up competing with this tenacious woman that I paid a hundred and five bucks for a blanket that I was going to hide as soon as I got home.

Keep your emotions out of it! When emotions go up, intelligence goes down. Business is no place for the ego's petty battles. Had I engaged that woman in conversation, maybe asked her why she wanted it, I might have discovered my mistake earlier. Instead, I was so determined to "stay the course" that I became myopic.

Imagine how that same dynamic plays itself out every day throughout the world when the stakes are far higher and more dangerous. Corporations often make decisions based on what the competition is doing, not because they have closely examined the facts and chosen what was achievable and sustainable.

Rule of Resolution #5: Shift your language and attention from problems to solutions; turn "why can't we . . . ?" into "how can we . . . ?"

When the stakes are high and the issues complex, you need to know how to use language the way a kendo master uses a samurai sword: not to cut others down but to create clear distinctions. Use language to steer clear of problems, and instead engage them in your picture of the solution. People look in the direction you move their focus.

I worked with an attorney who was a partner in a business. His partners were pushing him out, so he came to me and said, "Here are my demands."

I was looking at his list of demands thinking, this is like a hostage situation. He's got these guys captive and he's saying, "You get me these things, and I'll leave."

This is actually the typical approach people take in negotiations—and it is typically ineffective. Though they are not paying me to teach them more effective ways to negotiate, I let them know there are more effective ways to get what they want—ways that don't involve a standoff or all sides going on the attack.

To illustrate the importance of focusing on solutions, I asked him, "If I came to you as an attorney and said, 'Here are my demands,' what would be your first gut reaction?"

He said, "I'd say, 'Hell, no! You're not going to make demands of me.'"

"Exactly," I replied. "You're sounding the battle horn. So what do they do? They dig in their heels. Then everyone sets up their encampment, and the negotiations take forever. Watch out how you frame your thoughts. You want all these points, okay. But how can you let them know what you want in a way that doesn't make them push back?"

As a lawyer, he had no alternatives, so I suggested discussion points rather than a list of demands.

"I get where you're going with this," he said. "Make it more like a mediation."

I said, "Why not, if we can still get you want you want without the conflict?" He was a cancer survivor, so the less emotional stress, the better.

He said, "Okay, so I'd say, 'Why can't we have a provision that if I get sick, the buyout deal takes care of my wife?'"

I said, "Great. Better. Now, think from their perspective—what does it sound like if I pose the question by asking, 'Why can't we do this?'"

He got it. "They respond with all the reasons why they can't."

"Exactly," I said. "They respond to the way the question is posed. So instead, ask, "How *can* we do this?' It presupposes a viable way it *can* be done. It also puts both sides on the same side, focused on *how.*"

"Hmm, I never thought of that," he said.

He called me the next day and said, "That was the easiest negotiation I've ever been in!" And remember, he was an attorney. He was trained to be adversarial, so he was amazed at how effective collaborative language was.

To access free training and more resources go to:
www.theentrepreneurssolution.com/resources

CHAPTER 11

COLLABORATE

Partnering: People Who Need People—
Selling the Community Experience

The ability to deal with people is as purchasable a commodity as sugar or coffee,
and I will pay more for that ability than for any other under the sun.
—John D. Rockefeller

COLLABORATION = Partners + Innovation

L et's face it: people can be a real challenge at times. Bubbly one minute, stubborn the next, hard to read, moody, procrastinating—everyone's so different! That's exactly why the ability to deal with people, as John D. Rockefeller pointed out, is so valuable. Some entrepreneurs are daunted by the financial aspects of the company. Others shy away from innovation and marketing because they don't consider themselves "the creative type." But money minds and natural marketers can be hired. Your far more important concern is how to collaborate with colleagues, clients, contractors, and customers to generate loyalty and enthusiasm. This will make your company's success a team effort.

The best CEOs are the ones who bring out the best in individuals and at the same time galvanize the team around a common cause. Jack Welch, General Electric's immensely personable and dynamic CEO for twenty-five years, expected a great deal from his team leaders. And he wasn't shy about communicating what each one was doing great and what they needed to do better. He put a lot of stock in hiring the right person in the first place—one who matched his own level of drive and commitment. He was also legendary for rallying the whole company around the bigger picture: staying on the leading edge of innovation in technology. This is the range of ability in communication that great leaders usually manifest.

But can you become a people person if you're not one already? YES! If that's the one skill you learn from this book—how to play well with others—you are already *way* ahead of the game. Make your people feel important. And make the work environment feel fun if you can. I'm not talking about balloons in the meeting room where outside trainers keep your people from their jobs all day to tell them how to do their jobs. I'm talking about creating such a fun atmosphere that motivation and efficiency arise from a genuine desire to keep their job, not from the threat of losing it.

Zappos puts a great deal of creative energy into making the job fun. As a result, few employees want to work anywhere else. They prize their unique work environment, and therefore, their work ethic is a by-product of their personal investment in keeping a good thing and being proud of their results.

Everyone Is a Potential Partner

What's true for a company can be true for an entire country. Difficult times fraught with uncertainty or despair can push people apart or draw them together. If we continue to act as individuals, competing for limited resources, jobs, and money, we all suffer. But as partners, we all can create more opportunities and wealth together.

Running the country is necessarily a collaboration. The members of Congress would do well to take a lesson from the entrepreneurial thinking of NASA's Apollo 13 engineers, who refused to cave when faced with what looked like imminent disaster. That is how you want to innovate and collaborate in your business. Be realistic about the circumstances and the resources you have available, yet stay open to going beyond what has ever been done before. Bring in the right individuals, and be clear that you want them to pool their resources, to *collaborate*, not compete. When you focus several minds together, you think exponentially.

As you put together a team to share your dream, match the type with the task, and again, make sure you share ideals and intentions. In other words, surround yourself with the right people—people with (1) the right skills for the right job, and (2) values that match your company's core values.

Put Together a Team to Create the Dream

Clif Bar rewards its team well. But the rewards come as a result of being onboard with the values first. It's the meaning-first model of success. By now enough CEOs have tested it out that we can safely say it works.

Ample studies and experience have shown that the old-school method of hiring—asking every single candidate the same interview questions and comparing the answers—has never proved effective in finding the right person for the right job. Performance simply has little or no correlation with canned answers. Let your collaborations and your company practices reflect your identity. Collaborate in the same way that you connect—use empathy and language to understand others' deeper needs.

Match the Skills With the Job

Every individual will have a different piece of the puzzle. We've all seen those heist movies—one guy is the safecracker, another is the brilliant strategist, another is the charmer who works the door, and another is a bomb maker or the contortionist. Together, they can pull off anything. Setting aside the criminal objective, that is the way you want to feel in your company: that you've got it all covered. Even as the leader, you don't want to have to carry everyone—or anyone.

You hire those who carry their own weight and lead within their strengths. Only then does the company become greater than the sum of its parts.

Your success relies on your finding these "partners in crime." In the world of business, though, you will want to look for skills more along these lines:

- relater
- feeler
- thinker
- doer

Varieties of Human Archetypes

Each team member will have her or his own strengths and weaknesses. These are pretty broad categories, but the better you understand your people's needs and abilities, the better you will be able to make the most of these human resources:

Relater
- shows support and concern for others
- likes to help others and believes we all need help from time to time
- gives personal recognition for achievement
- is empathetic and understanding
- is informal and personal
- is flexible and keeps the door open
- is not demanding
- needs regular personal contact
- doesn't push too hard for immediate action or change
- is NOT suited for jobs that require precision, in-depth analysis, or fast action
- Is not good at meeting deadlines

Feeler
- is creative, visionary, and able to identify links among concepts
- is an innovative problem solver
- has a long-term view of things

- is future oriented
- is "big picture" oriented
- relies on an "intellectual approach"
- is not action oriented; does not necessarily relate well with a wide variety of people
- is the "warm, touchy-feely" type
- is NOT aggressive, domineering, or demanding
- is NOT especially pragmatic or down-to-earth

Thinker

- is logical and well organized
- is specific and detail oriented
- ties past results and present concerns with short-term future potential
- stresses facts, evidence, background, and details
- needs explicit directions and adequate time to produce quality results
- does not appreciate overly domineering supervision
- does not like to cut corners to save time
- does not work well in crisis situations that require quick decisions based on incomplete information
- is not driven by emotional or sentimental stimuli

Doer

- talks in terms of plans, results, and change
- is specific and to the point
- likes to be commended for her energy, drive, competitiveness, quick actions
- stresses action plans with short-term deadlines
- does not appreciate long, detailed meetings
- does not generally focus on long-range objectives
- is generally not overly organized, logical, or rational
- does not appreciate ambiguity or a lot of information at once
- does not generally dwell in the world of ideas, is not overly concerned with the question "why?"

In general, what a person does best is also what he or she enjoys most. The more you can match team members' abilities with their responsibilities, the greater their sustainability. If you add to their job description tasks that play into their weaknesses, it will be a struggle for both of you. They may eventually burn out, and you will be disappointed or frustrated with their performance.

Collaborating With Colleagues

Influence is the impact we have on others. It is measured not only at the end of the fiscal year but daily. Your influence will be far reaching if you create mutually beneficial relationships with those who can extend your reach, contribute to your brand, get your message across, execute, and deliver. Leading others is more about engagement than about compliance. Consider your staff and coworkers collaborative partners in your dreams.

For one, appreciate them. Don't end up being a cattle driver. When you feel desperate, it's easy to start pushing people to do what you want them to, rather than trusting them to do it. Shift your focus from forcing productivity to forming real relationships, and don't underestimate how much an atmosphere of appreciation and acknowledgment can improve productivity. If you foster competition among the team members, it can—and probably will—backfire. They will spend more time jockeying for position and currying favor from the boss—you—than collaborating to create new products and plans to succeed together.

Collaboration doesn't mean loss of control, as some fear. It means greater brainpower. Wouldn't you rather cultivate a culture of collaboration, where everyone has a stake in achieving the greater mission? Recognize each member's contribution, large or small. From that level of engagement comes a more powerful communal willingness, drive, and level of accountability.

Trust is also important. Transparency is key. In a recent survey, Interaction Associates found that business performance over a five-year period was directly correlated to the organizational trust that existed. Indeed, nothing long-lasting can be created without it. Your team members need to know that you trust them. Generally, people don't want to disappoint those who are counting on them. When you let your team know you expect great things from them, you give them the path to rise to those expectations. And the converse is also true: your partners need to know they can trust you, too. They want to know you are who you say you are, and they need to know that you've got their back. If they fear being betrayed or hurt in some way, you'll never get to experience their fullest potential, because they will always be holding back.

In my twenties, when I was studying karate in Japan, my roommate and I trained and lived together. We had a bond. But I didn't realize how strong that bond was until my bike accident landed me in the hospital. I hadn't seen him in two or more years. And yet, he was ready to get on a plane the next day, to be by my side. Our bond of trust had formed because, in training, every time I gave him my arm he had the option to break it, yet he didn't. This kind of relationship forms when everyone is working toward a common high goal. One of the first lessons of karate is that you have to trust your training partner in every moment. When you are being real, your trustworthiness is conveyed through your true character (which includes your actions), through your internal congruence, and through your communication. Miraculous levels of success happen in an atmosphere of trust.

Collaborating With Customers

Jeff Bezos invested an initial forty thousand dollars into his idea of starting an online bookstore, and in 1994 Amazon was born in his garage. It was doing well enough, but it made a bigger leap in sales when he had the idea to let his customers write their own book reviews. It differentiated his business in a personal and meaningful way to his buyers. An amazing phenomenon happened: they got more emotionally invested in the company site, they started coming back to do repeat business, and they started telling others about it. His online bookstore quickly turned into something more akin to an online *community*. He was selling the human connection and building his business in the process. The collaboration with his customers brought Amazon to $15.7 million within those first three years.

Collaborating With Other Companies

When Amazon threw open the shop doors to sell CDs, DVDs, electronics, and home improvement items, toys, and other things, sales shot up to a billion dollars by 1999. Then the business took a dive. The company was hemorrhaging profits. It had to scale back on costs and staff. This is when Bezos had his next big company-saving idea: collaborate with other companies. Toys R Us, Target, and other popular retailers recognized a mutually beneficial connection when they saw it. They all collaborated to make one of the biggest virtual commercial portals in all cyberspace. Today, with the acquisition of Zappos, Amazon is worth almost $141.9 billion and growing. Even among American brick-and-mortar retailers, as of 2013, only Wal-Mart had a higher market cap.

Open your eyes to the partnering possibilities. Rather than be threatened by your competition, look at how you can create connections and collaborative partnerships. Innovation at this scale makes anything possible.

Competitive Partnerships

Collaboration is not necessarily the opposite of competition. Healthy competition can form dynamic relationships that I call "competitive partnerships." Competitive partnerships exist within sports teams and even families. As siblings and as teammates, we compare ourselves to those closest to us to define ourselves more clearly and differentiate our traits. The same occurs in business: we hone our own identity and constantly seek to improve our performance, to stand out. The best part of competition is that it motivates us to sharpen our skills and stay on our toes.

The fact that Apple exists, for example, makes Microsoft a better company, and vice versa. Apple's focus is not to destroy Microsoft (as far as I know). It is to provide products that are innovative, creative, and desired by the community. Having "rival" companies on its tail forces Microsoft to think and rethink how it can differentiate its products, its market, and its marketing.

If the focus is *how do I destroy my competition?* then we're back on the grade school playground or in politics, where so much energy goes into making "the other side" look bad that little is left over for collaborating on solutions to real problems. That's a lose-lose for everybody. If you doubt this, just take a good, hard look at how Congress conducts business.

The New Entrepreneur and the Collaborative Economy

The new entrepreneur has higher personal standards. The new entrepreneur is out there trying new models and financial systems and asking, *how can we all grow together? How do we all create something that we can share and that will sustain us all?* They are more self-referential in their convictions and, therefore, less susceptible to the ego's tendency toward greed. The new entrepreneurs are creating their own paradigms for sustainable success in every respect. They know there is enough to go around. And they recognize that their success relies on a thriving culture. They are aware of their influence, so they align their corporate decisions with the win-win-wins they envision.

Wealth without greed is possible. We're ready for a collaborative economy based on healthy competitive partnerships. None of us can do it on our own, and the same old business models are no longer the answer. Be clear in what you stand for, and others will come to collaborate with you.

> To access free training and more resources go to:
> **www.theentrepreneurssolution.com/resources**

CHAPTER 12

INNOVATION: CREATING SUSTAINABILITY— REINVENTING THE WHEEL

The relationship we have with our people and the culture
of our company is our most sustainable competitive advantage.
—**Howard Shultz**

COLLABORATION = Partners + Innovation

S ustainability is not just about recycling anymore. It's about *rethinking* what lasts. *What is regenerative? What is needed for us all to live a better life?*

We like to say, "Money makes the world go around," but obviously, we make the money go around, and we need to take responsibility for *how* we make it go around. Money doesn't move anywhere on its own. Ideas make the world go around, and you make the ideas. To invest in our future, we need to commit to sustainability as the ideal that we build all our new ideas on. This begins with rethinking every assumption we have ever made about the purpose and function of money and business. It's safe to say that some of the ways we do business now and in the past is, for the most part, not healthy for the environment or the economy. When such a large portion of our national economy is based on speculation, we only have wilder and more uncomfortable roller coaster rides to look forward to. We claim that we want a prosperous and stable economy even as we continue to build our future over a sinkhole. We know it will inevitably suck everything down, but we keep our fingers crossed hoping it will devastate other people, not us. That's not only short-term thinking at its worst. It's also "I'm just in this for myself" thinking, which excludes any possibility for fulfillment. The strongest economies and businesses in the world are built on industry and innovation. We knew that once. Now that we have a model for collaborative partnerships, it's time now to reinvent the wheel of fortune, with everyone in mind.

Innovating New Business Models

Today's companies need constant R & D to sustain their success in unpredictable, fast-changing markets. But I've found that some entrepreneurs are intimidated by the notion of having to be innovative. They assume that they have to be some kind of Einstein, who gets a flash of genius, or a Thomas Edison, who spends years tirelessly experimenting to come up with some never-before-seen technology. Innovation is really just about understanding the needs of your market and keeping pace. Sometimes it's just reworking an old idea to make it relevant in today's culture. Sometimes it's providing solutions to needs or desires before people even realize they have them.

In the Age of Information, it was the companies that moved information more efficiently—CNN, Microsoft, Kinko's, FedEx, and Google, to name but a few—that made their millions and billions. Whether they or the public created the need is debatable. All they really did was make existing systems faster and more efficient. News used to run from six to seven p.m., then again at eleven; Ted Turner just made it run twenty-four hours.

Now, as we enter the Age of Connection, the biggest opportunities lie in fulfilling people's need to feel human again. Even as we extend our virtual reach through our Internet connections, there is still a sense of disconnection. As we gain the freedom to work away from the workplace, we miss the human interaction. People are searching for ways to regain a sense of belonging and community. That's why companies such as Amazon, Barnes and Noble, Starbucks, Facebook, MySpace, and YouTube are capitalizing on their creations of new communal spaces, real and virtual. People from all over the globe come together now with their like-minded extended "family" or, as some call it, their "tribe."

As the culture demands constant growth, our entrepreneurial mind needs to evolve at an accelerated pace. We need to innovate new ways to solve the issues as we create them. I coined the term "sustainable success" to describe the new business models that entrepreneurs are creating now to fulfill society's compounding needs for sustainability in the Age of Connection. Cutting-edge companies are looking beyond what is, to what must be. It's time to go beyond asking what is possible and go for the *im*possible.

"One for One," and One for All

Beyond inventing new products, the companies thriving in the twenty-first century are actually reinventing the way they do business.

You could say Blake Mycoskie sells shoes, but then, so does Zappos, yet the two could not have more divergent business models. While both were customized to serve their market's shifting needs and values, their business models have everything to do with the respective CEOs' intentions and ideals. Tony Hsieh's intention was to become the biggest shoe provider, with the widest variety of shoes, delivered the fastest, all while creating a community for his team and his customers. His ideal was fulfillment in both senses of the word: he wanted to fulfill his own need to be challenged, as well as to create an overnight order fulfillment that would wow the customer with its efficiency and speed. Toward that end, Hsieh set his financial goals high, and he based the retail online distribution center within fifteen minutes of the UPS Worldport hub.

Meanwhile, Mycoskie's primary intention was to make the world a better place. An entrepreneur since the age of nineteen, he had already established several successful start-ups: an ad agency, a reality television network, and an online driver's education course for teens. His inspiration to start selling shoes came to him while he was traveling through Argentina, where he saw children who had developed diseases and deformities for lack of shoes. Mycoskie saw firsthand how happy the children were to receive a pair of shoes from a local volunteer organization, but it was obvious that they would soon grow out of them and need more shoes. In one "aha!" moment, he decided to combine his talent for turning a profit with his desire to help kids. Mycoskie developed the "one for one" business model: For every pair of shoes sold, he would give another pair to a child somewhere in the world. This is where the slogan and, eventually, the name TOMS came from: "shoes for tomorrow." Despite having no experience in philanthropy, he figured that business and philanthropy were not so different—after all, both boiled down to fulfilling a need.

Spurred ahead by his own desire to improve on a situation where he saw lack, Blake Mycoskie created unique solutions and took the risk to make it happen. TOMS has now expanded its reach into several other countries and given a million pairs of new shoes to children in twenty-five countries, and counting.

Creating Sustainability

The many accepted lines of authority in the corporate environment and in our nation's model for doing business and finance stifle the entrepreneur's natural inclination to seek change and improvement. As a result, the very system that could benefit most from innovation can't yet see its way clear of the old, dysfunctional model. We could be thriving again economically if we stopped waiting on solutions to come from the government or other outside sources and instead cultivated our nation's entrepreneurial resolve.

Five Domains of Innovation

When we think about innovation the focus is on doing something differently not new or improved. Here is what I mean. Improvements are not really innovations they are simply tweaks that change the look and feel and maybe some functionality in a minor way. This will not move the needle in great ways in the market place. If we are looking at doing things in a totally new "never been done before" way, that is more about invention versus innovation. Innovation is really focused on doing things differently though. When you think about innovation you need to strip away the past way of doing things to allow you to come from an open-minded place of zero-based thinking. Here are the five domains for innovation in any business:

1. product and service
2. marketing
3. business model
4. management and company culture
5. product delivery and process

How could you change the way you do business within each of these five domains? Get creative. And consider the possibility that you can change lives for the better in the process.

1. Product and Service

It sounds more like a "note to self" Bill Gates should have made, but Apple has been just as culpable as Microsoft of moving forward so quickly that its services have trouble keeping pace with its creations.

Innovative products often come as a happy result of a mistake. And more often than not, they come as a hard-won result of tenacity and perseverance. Take masking tape, for example. Dick Drew worked as a researcher for 3M in the 1920s when all the company manufactured was abrasives, such as sandpaper. Drew happened to be a problem-solver, though, and a stubborn one at that. He didn't let corporate policy stand in the way of his solution-oriented mind. Walking into an auto body shop one day to test a new batch of sandpaper, he heard some workers cursing. To his alert ears, it was a cry for help—a sure sign of a need to be remedied. Sure enough, the workers were upset because every time they pulled the tape off a car they had just freshly painted, it peeled off some of their new paint job, too. Drew immediately busied his brain—and his office hours—with creating just the right type of adhesive for the job. Despite his boss's direct orders to stop wasting his time and get back to his job of improving sandpaper, Drew persisted, even cleverly devising a way to spend unapproved company funds on developing a paper-making machine that would eventually produce the first masking tape. As a $92.1 billion company today, 3M now understands that innovation is the only way to sustain its edge in the market.

Today the official corporate policy is, *"If you have the right person on the right project, and they are absolutely dedicated to finding a solution, leave them alone. Tolerate their initiative and trust them."*

2. Marketing

Getting others to buy into TOMS brand—the marketing side of the biz—is innovative yet surprisingly simple and straightforward, like Mycoskie himself and his product. The company's message is, *"You're not just buying another pair of shoes for yourself—you're helping someone somewhere else in the world."* This marketing engages and appeals to "the new consumer," who still wants to have fun shopping for shoes but considers it a bonus if their consuming habits also benefit others around the world.

When we want to make sure that consumer and corporate ideals are aligned, intelligence gathering is key on both sides of the buying equation. As a company, it will help to understand and keep track of your market's shifting ideals. Amazon software tracks its customers' preferences. If that's too expensive, you can use blogs, videos, comment pages, or reviews to find niche markets and better understand their interests and desires. These are just a few of the new tools that can generate leads for your company. The Internet is now the way to keep your ear to the ground and know what's coming around the bend.

3. Business Model

TOMS Shoes' "one for one" business model is a great example of innovating while forming the company. Blake Mycoskie's invention was born of necessity and inspiration: "As an entrepreneur, I always wanted to incorporate giving somehow in my business, but never could find the right way to do so. TOMS allows me to mix my two passions—business and philanthropy—and prove that they are no longer mutually exclusive. I only hope to inspire others to do the same: find their passion and pursue it."

Mycoskie has even achieved his goal of inspiring others. Several companies have adopted his unique business model, to the point where the new "one for one" business model has become something of a trend, with celebrity-supported events such as www.onedaywithoutshoes.com.

Another new trend is the collaborative partnership model in which companies generate profit by using each other's platform and product. For instance, app developers make a full 70 percent of profits from the thousands of apps they offer. Apple keeps 30 percent for "lending" its platform. It's a symbiotic relationship in which the apps feed off the platform and the platform benefits from each app's success. In 2013, Apple announced that more than 50 billion apps have been downloaded. This model is a great example of interdependent autonomy.

4. Management and Company Culture

Plenty is changing within today's physical work environment to improve the psychological environment, from spa treatments and scooters on "campus" to ergonomic comfort and yoga stations, where employees can get horizontal during their breaks. Workspaces are being designed to unleash more creative, right-brain thinking. Toyota and other companies employ graduates with degrees in environmental design to create office space and furniture, even taking into account the feng shui of the place. Microsoft consulted feng shui specialists in designing its campus, where employees and executives alike get from meeting to meeting on scooters.

Probably the biggest change that has occurred in the vast area of management is a total overhaul of the old way of "managing" workers. It's called "results-only work environment, or ROWE, in which people are paid for their productivity, not for their time spent on the clock. It was the innovation of Cali Ressler and Jody Thompson, two human-resource managers who worked at BestBuy and are now entrepreneurs or, as they call themselves, "change agents," with their own massive consulting business. Instead of trying to control employee performance, the company gives complete control to the employees to use their time as they see fit, as long as they hit their goals and deadlines and get the final result. By employing this innovative management style, companies are seeing average productivity increases of 35 percent. As a secondary benefit, ROWE exposes a team's underperformers, the ones who normally get away with contributing less, while retaining those who are self-motivated.

5. Product Delivery and Process

Nike now lets us design our own sneakers, while Red Robin encourages us to customize our burger online. Those product delivery strategies really keep the picky customer happy. And for those consumers whom I would call "discerning," there are myriad choices of hotels that won't waste water washing your sheets and towels if you tell them not to, new housecleaning companies that use only environmentally friendly cleaning products if that's what you prefer, and a whole new line of cars (finally) that can alternate between electric and gas power, depending on your choice that day.

Patagonia has long been a role model in this respect. While it may not have reached zero impact yet, it has invested a great deal and made great strides. After creating a whole new global market for organic cotton, CEO and innovator Yvon Chouinard realized that the increased demand was causing some negative repercussions. He wanted instead to invent a whole new material that could get closer to 100 percent sustainability. Here he recalls just how much his team had to rethink everything in order to reinvent one thing: "We didn't have any of the answers. There was no book you could pick up and say, 'Here's what we need to do.' We didn't know that making clothes out of a synthetic was better than making them out of a natural material. And so what about rayon? It's made out of cellulose, which is made out of trees—that seems like a good product. But then you find out they use really toxic chemicals to convert it."

They looked at hemp and wool and found too many disadvantages that were "damaging as hell." Conventionally grown cotton was such an environmental nightmare that he said, "To know this and not switch to organic cotton would be unconscionable." At some point, though, it became apparent that even organic cotton was a waste of resources. A corporate partner in Japan then innovated a process in which polyester could be recycled like aluminum cans into a new type of fabric, so that no new material needed to be added.

This is how far Chouinard was willing to go down the rabbit hole to find out what is possible and how we can sustain ourselves long into the future. In the end, he admits, "Patagonia will never be completely socially responsible. It will never make a totally sustainable, nondamaging product. But it is committed to trying."

If we are not keeping our fingers on the pulse and being creative and innovative and understanding what our consumer and our marketplace ultimately wants, then we lose our financial sustainability and we lose our relevance.

Implementation and Feedback

The last two pieces of the innovation puzzle are implementation and feedback. These are integral and ongoing. To execute the production and marketing plan and finally go to market would seem the last step in the process. But this is actually the *middle* of the experiment, because now we wait to hear back from our customers. They are our testers. They are happy to tell us what we've done right and what we've done wrong, and they provide this service free.

Do you remember the scene in *Apollo 13* when Gary Sinise's character climbs into the simulation capsule to test the device that the engineers innovated? He tells them what will work for those astronauts and what won't. It's such a long, arduous process of problem solving that at one point, the team tells Sinise's character that he can take a break if he wants to, and he says, "They don't get a break; I don't get a break. Let's keep going." Though he didn't get to go up on the Apollo 13 mission, he played just as vital a role in his team's successful return.

This is how your clients and customers will become your partners in innovation. Look at your product or service from every angle of the user's experience: *What's good about this? What works here? What doesn't work there? What can we improve? What can we give them as a bonus to exceed their expectations?*

And don't be afraid to adjust your new innovation or toss it away and start over. Fulfilling their needs can fulfill yours.

To access free training and more resources go to:
www.theentrepreneurssolution.com/resources

CHAPTER 13

CAPITALIZE

Perception: PROVIDE Your LURE

*If you want to succeed, you should strike out on new paths
rather than travel the worn paths of accepted success.*
—**John D. Rockefeller**

CAPITALIZING = Perception + Monetizing

I t's not enough to innovate great products and profit-generating ways to deliver on those ideas—you have to *let others know* (a) what you have accomplished and (b) how it will make their lives better. This is sometimes called the *value proposition*. Then, of course, capitalize on that mutually beneficial relationship. How? First, stop thinking only in terms of developing your product or service and start thinking A LOT about the *perception* of your product/service/company.

Rising to the top in your field, getting repeat customers, the phone ringing off the hook, money piling up in the accounts, you on the cover of *Forbes* magazine for making the list of the world's richest people—it all starts with a perception. Ultimately, yes, it is about delivery, credibility, and quality. It goes without saying—or, at least, it had better!—that we must promote the truth and overdeliver on our promises.

This is Marketing 101. Unlike in politics, where constituents vote once every two to four years, customers vote every day or every time they need something. So, unlike a politician, you have to back up your claims—right now and every time. If the product is not what they *perceived* it would be, you lose customers, longevity, and sustainability. For the sake of integrity and profitability, you *have* to deliver on your claims.

Get Your Market's Attention

Capitalizing on your product is simple as long as you understand human buying decisions, which is to say, it's simple but not always easy. Humans are complex. They are rarely congruent. Some things appeal to their ego but not their values. They want social acceptance, but they want to be considered unique individuals. They prize status and also sustainability. Now add that what they want changes continually based on their life stages. What mattered so much suddenly just isn't that important anymore. We all have a lot of innate contradictions to contend with, heaped on top of cultural changes—perhaps more now than ever—as we all try to break old habits and form healthier ones for our future. Still, you can make a strong positive connection with your market.

And, of course, you have your product or service. You will build your market's perception on your company's performance. So marketing is about making personal connections with more and more people. Think of "them" as more than your "market"; think of them as YOU—what do *you* want, like, buy, resonate with. What would you need to know to be true about this company in order to understand its credibility, performance, values, and culture? Whatever is appealing to you will likely have the same effect on "them."

To generate a compelling perception, associate your offering with what they want, not with what they don't *want.*

And remember, you have several chances to appeal to buyers, on several levels and in several aspects of your business. Most business gurus talk about marketing, or branding, your product in terms of "differentiation." To me, that sounds as if you have to make your product do something totally different from anything else on the market. It's more about how to get people's attention and appeal to them on an almost visceral level. So differentiating yourself in the marketplace boils down to creating the perception of your product first and making sure it is aligned with the prospective buyers' *self*-perception—that is, their *identity, ideals,* and *intentions.* Your product or service needs to be aspirational as much as it needs to be useful. Translation:

- *Who do your prospective buyers think they are?*
- *What's important to them?*
- *What do they want out of life?*

I like to refer to buyers as "investors" because, despite all appearances, they aren't just spending money. On a deeper level, they are investing in themselves. Any decision to let go of their hard-earned cash must hinge on whether they see what the product gives back as worth more than the price. A book or an app could give back to them hours or days of downtime and escape from other stresses, so it's "worth" the twenty-dollar cost. A laptop with Internet access could give them contacts all over the world for their business, so two thousand dollars is a drop in the bucket compared to the money it will give back. A five-thousand-dollar education in all aspects of business could make them a hundred times that. It's all about investing in what's important to them.

Make a Good Impression: PROVIDE Your LURE

In Part One, you clarified your own sense of identity and discovered what types of ideals are meaningful to you. Now you need to understand your buyers' personal identity and ideals and why your product is meaningful to *them*! Use every contact point you make as an opportunity to toss out your LURE. Your lure is the long-lasting, unique, relatable, enticing impression you make on them:

- Long-lasting
- Unique
- Relatable
- Enticing

Differentiate yourself and capitalize on your communication skills by consciously crafting a clear message in these six areas of your business:

- **Perception**
- **Relationship**
- **Offer**
- **Value Exchange**
- **ID**/Identification with a personality
- **Experience**

1. PERCEPTION

Perfect example: I hate to burst anyone's bubble, but an iPod is simply an MP3 player. It was not new technology, and there were already tons of them on the market. Why did Apple suddenly influence a massive buy-in with the iPod?

Because people are committed to their *identity* and *ideals*. According to Apple's billboards, to buy an iPod was to get everything that was important in their targeted buyers' life—they were free; they were dancing in the streets to the beat of their own drummer. Apple's billboards didn't even use print or the product name. All you had to see was the silhouette of some very cool cats rocking out with wires dangling from their ears connected to a tiny, thin rectangle in their hand. Walking around with an iPod meant individuality, whereas PC meant uniformity. Apple displayed a brilliant attunement to the zeitgeist of its niche market. This is truly about actualizing your idealistic self.

The old school of thought holds that your product equals your company's value. In the new school, perception backed by realized customer expectations equals value. Selling is not so much about product as about perception.

As a caveat, in this age of total exposure through Facebook, Twitter, YouTube, and other media, be aware of the overall perception sent out through *all* portals of information, beyond just your personal and business interactions. Manage the big-picture perception.

2. RELATIONSHIP

Clients ask me sometimes, "When do you start bringing in that emotional contact when dealing with the customer?" I'm still surprised by the question because of its underlying assumption that you have to be distant to be professional. In my experience, it's just the opposite: when you make it personal, you don't just have customers, you have meaningful partnerships. In our closest friendships and relationships, we look for ways to support the dreams of those we care about. We tell them what we appreciate about them, and we listen when they need to work through a problem. By thinking of yourself as having the same role in your business relationships, you can build stronger customer loyalty.

Don't just make contacts; make connections. Your business relationships can become a big part of what makes work fulfilling, if you let them.

Also, as you create your marketing plan, consider your company's relationship to the planet. Let everyone know how you or your service or product contribute to humanity, the environment, or some other important issue. Several retail sites generate more business by donating a percentage of their sales to a cause or selling merchandise made in developing countries. Plenty of catalogs give holiday shoppers the opportunity to double and triple their giving by buying an item made in a developing country, or giving to a nonprofit in someone else's name. Positioning your company by what it contributes to the world at large gives your product or service more meaning and puts you in a larger context, with greater possibilities to grow exponentially. By conveying the unique role you have taken on with sustainability, you can grow your business very effectively customer by customer, or you can pitch that LURE further out, to a larger community.

3. OFFER

Ultimately, the offer you make needs to have a compelling pull with your clients or customers. Your offer can be structured in many different ways including providing a portion of your product or service at low or no cost. The key is to make it compelling from an emotional perspective.

Have you noticed how the best things in life now really *are* free? Google, Craigslist, YouTube, Facebook, Skype, and now Shazam—well, free to a point. I got this Shazam app from Jeremy for every time I heard a song I liked. Using the app it would listen to the song and give you the title, artist and album of the song in seconds. After five songs, I got a message saying essentially, "You reached your limit. If you want more, you need to upgrade." Brilliant! I went for it because the company had innovated a way to serve a universal need—we all drive ourselves crazy when we can't think of the title of a particular song we like. Now the app also gives you lyrics, artist tour information and even allows you to purchase the song directly from your iPhone.

There are several different ways to create an offer. The next chapter will show you how to set up your offer in a way that creates the perception that the buyers are getting far more value than they are paying for. Here I want to get you thinking about how you can catch customers' attention right off the bat by giving away your product or service "free." In fact, the word "free" is so eye-catchingly popular, you now have to write it as "Fr**ee" just to bypass the software that sends those unsolicited sales e-mails into the spam folder.

The "services for free, upgrade for a fee" offer is nothing new. Little cubes of muffins on bakery countertops, toothpaste samples in your junk mail, tiny cups of frothy, sweet drinks passed out by baristas—every business should have its own equivalent of the sample tray.

People are generally set in their buying habits. But "free" remains one of the most enticing, attractive words in the English language. Giving someone the chance to try out your product or service is an effective marketing tool to build familiarity and loyalty. It is one of the most tried-and-true techniques to get customers over their resistance to change.

With the free offer, companies, gaming sites, and membership sites such as LinkedIn and Match.com get you at a low price point, then offer you tiered pricing, with your cost rising as your benefits increase. This type of offer gathers potential paying customers in droves. Once they are committed to paying even a small amount—and companies offer low monthly payments to maintain the perception of being a good buy—customers are much more likely to "upgrade."

"Upgrade" is a much more attractive word than "pay" or "cost" to use in your marketing. Create some type of tiered system that easily moves your buyers up the scale of investing in more valuable benefits for them. It's a nice way to give them a wide range of choices, all of which further their success in some way.

4. VALUE EXCHANGE

Value exchange is such an important part of monetizing an idea that the entire next chapter is dedicated to it. But I will explain the concept here so you can think about how to differentiate yourself in this area. An astonishing number of businesses limit their growth potential by never understanding the true value of what they offer. The idea of value exchange is simple: *what do they get in exchange for what they give?* People will buy only when they perceive the value of what they give up as less than the value of what they get, and people will sell only when they perceive the value of what they sell as less than the value of what they receive in payment.

So your first job as entrepreneur and CEO is to understand the potential benefits the customer will receive. But beyond the customer it is equally significant to define what you're your team and your vendors will receive as a result of getting into a relationship with you. Even more important, you must then clearly translate the *value* of those benefits in the following terms (and perhaps others as well):

- financial return
- mental or emotional benefit
- impact on lifestyle
- physical comfort
- business or personal productivity
- love, connectedness, and popularity

The value of a product, service, or company is its *perceived* value. It can change based on the economy (obviously), the company's reputation (perception), and current relevance (perception)—any of which can skyrocket or tank based on the buzz on the streets that day.

Valuation consulting for businesses is one area of expertise from which I make a great living. My offer appears to be based on my knowledge of finance, business, and law. And yet, the true value of what I do comes down to my understanding of psychology, while the benefits I offer my clients amount to my ability to communicate and resolve issues for them. The financial and psychological value of what they receive—peace of mind and satisfaction—is equal to or greater than the monetary value they give me. If it weren't, they wouldn't invest in my service.

Traditionally, employers and employees alike went by the notion that raises were based on time served rather than value provided. You were paid for time spent at the office, and got a raise based on putting in overtime. This set up a "*my time versus company* time" paradigm, which called for a lot of personal sacrifices and led to a sort of split personality in which you had to be one person at work, then someone else at home. This amounted to enforced incongruence.

For the new entrepreneur, *perceived value* is money. It doesn't matter how much time you take to do the job. What matters are the knowledge, experience, skills, personality, relationships, contacts, and potential business you bring to your customers and clients. Your monetary value is in the significance of the impact you have on others, emotionally or monetarily: how much your presentation increases their productivity and profit, the size of the contracts you can bring in, what they can turn around and charge for the information you just gave them, and so on.

- You need to understand the full value of the benefits you are giving, on several levels, before your market can understand it. Knowing your greater value will reflect directly in your earnings and impact.

5. ID: IDENTIFIABLE PERSONALITY

Personalities associated with your company make a great LURE. Sir Richard Branson is Virgin. He is an adventurer who almost never stops smiling. It's no accident, then, that almost all his products carry with them the association of living large and having fun. Perfumes or colognes with names like "Curious," "Instinct," and "Lovely" would not go anywhere without the faces of Britney Spears, David Beckham, and Sarah Jessica Parker in the ad, and all the desired traits they exude. Even animals can make great identifiable VIPs. The gecko that represents Geico Insurance is laid back, clever, and relatable. And Morris the cat was memorable whether or not you loved him for his snooty attitude. When the Chihuahua for Taco Bell died, it made national news. Animals can make a great *long-lasting, unique, relatable, enticing* impression.

Consider putting your own face and persona out there in your community. Start a blog that exudes personality. Brainstorm as many ways as you can to make your business personal.

6. EXPERIENCE

- Cirque du Soleil: Exciting! Sensual. Visually stimulating. Awe-inspiring.
- Craigslist: Simple. Straightforward. Communal. A welcome relief from flashy, in-your-face ads.
- Carl's Jr.: Juicy. Decadent. Anti-PC. Liberating.
- Caesar's Pizza: "Hot and fast."

At Disneyland, everything is a show. You don't see the characters out of character. The entire customer experience is managed.

My newfound loyalty to the coffee shop "It's a Grind" was based entirely on my positive first experience there. It's one thing to swing by the drive-through and pick up a cup of coffee. It's an altogether different, warm, fuzzy experience to come into a homey atmosphere where people know your name. It's more meaningful and memorable.

What experience does your company provide? Make it felt. Appeal to the visual, auditory, and kinesthetic senses: sight, sound, and touch. The more that technology distances us, the more we crave engagement. Give people more levels, *more dimensions*, on which to remember you.

To access free training and more resources go to:
www.theentrepreneurssolution.com/resources

CHAPTER 14

MONETIZING: CAPITALIZE, DON'T COMMODITIZE

Consumers are not loyal to cheap commodities.
They crave the unique, the remarkable and the human.
—Seth Godin

CAPITALIZING = Perception + Monetizing

Price Your Value; Capitalize on Your Product.

The importance of recognizing the right distinctions between your *product* and your *commodity* cannot be overstressed. You need to understand what you are *producing* versus what you are *selling*. Know the difference between what you offer and its benefit. Then go one step further to market its emotional and monetary value to a wide audience.

At Clif Bar, for example, the health bars are a commodity as well as a value. What the company offers is also what it represents. When I asked Gary Erickson what the value of his health bars is, he crystallized the distinction in one word: "There are probably a lot of words I can think of, but one would be 'lifestyle'—a balanced and happy lifestyle. That goes for the people who work for us, for the community that we support, and for the planet aspiration . . . it's the healthy lifestyle."

The Value of Your Business Lies in People's Values.

And now here's a little Economics 101. When we are willing to drop ten dollars for coffee and a pastry, we are living in a value exchange economy. We're clearly not just paying for the beans, sugar, milk, flour, and cream cheese. They aren't worth that much as commodities. As consumers, we are buying into the benefits of the beans, sugar, and milk: the quick pick-me-up, the warm atmosphere, the place to work, or whatever it is we personally get out of the experience. Starbucks sells experience. We perceive the value as greater than the dollar amount we're paying, while Starbucks is thinking the same thing: that it's getting more dollar value back than it is spending."

Perceived value is the reason why houses that brought half a million dollars last year are worth only a quarter million now, and why people pay ten thousand dollars a year to belong to a country club. It's only because they consider it worth *more* than ten thousand in relaxation and health, or perhaps because it's a ten-thousand-dollar investment in their business that yields million-dollar business contacts in the clubhouse. Either way, it's a worthwhile return on investment for them. So value is 100 percent in the individual buyer's mind. Your job is to communicate that value clearly based on what is important to your buyers—their values—and price the product or service accordingly.

An Accountant Is an Accountant Is an Accountant . . . Right?

Commodities, on the other hand, are goods given a universal price because they are considered qualitatively equivalent—for example, corn, coffee beans, oil, copper . . . accountants.

Historically, accountants have commoditized everything they do, because they themselves don't fully understand the value they can bring. They devalue their own currency in the consumer's mind until the presumption is that all accountants do is crunch numbers. Therefore, most accountants are treated as commodities with no significant qualitative differences. The same goes for most cable guys, customer service reps, insurance agents, real estate appraisers, and, in the past, teachers. Only now are some schools affirming the higher value exchange and setting their pay scale and rewards systems based on student results. If you are in a commoditized business, you have to work extra hard to differentiate yourself in the public's eyes.

Position Your Company in the Market.

First off, it bears repeating that *perceived* credibility MUST be followed by *actual* delivery, credibility, and quality. After creating a perception of value, you had better follow up with results. Not delivering, or underdelivering will kill an otherwise sustainable business every time.

When I opened my own firm, I knew I would need to back up my claims with consistent quality, over time. I strove to exceed expectations and earn a pristine reputation. To build that reputation and positioning as an authority, I began speaking around the country. I started writing articles. As a way to get even better at it, I began teaching what I knew. I created a whole series of CDs and offered them on my website. In other words, when firms needed a valuation expert, I made sure they had plenty of reasons to choose me. I positioned myself as a leading expert, and in the process, I became one.

To position your own company where you want to be in the marketplace, use the Four-Point Positioning System:

- Frame
- Campaign
- Deliver
- Serve

1. Frame Your Value.

Frame your value as you would frame up a camera shot: compose it in a way that draws attention to its most attractive features. I was advising a group of doctors who were trying to promote to other doctors a weekend seminar on how they could increase their practice. The seminar's price point was set at $3,200. The promoters' quandary was that so far, they had only twenty-five registered participants, and they needed at least forty to get back what they paid for the room. Their proposed plan was to drop the price to $2,000 to bring the other fifteen participants in.

I told them this tactic would accomplish just the opposite of what they wanted. Those who had already paid would question the seminar's value and demand a refund. Lowering the price only devalued the seminar's offer, which would lower its perceived value. The current ticket price wasn't the issue. The real issue was that potential buyers who were still on the fence needed to be convinced that they would get higher value than the current price.

But as I talked with the doctors, it became evident that they didn't even understand the value of their own information. They were so conditioned to think in terms of hourly office visit prices, it took a little convincing to get them to see what they were *really* offering.

They were teaching other doctors how to do toxicity analysis on their patients. So I asked them, "How much is it worth for a doctor to know how to do that?"

They said, "Each care plan is four thousand dollars."

I said, "So if one of your participants sells twelve care plans to her patients at four thousand each, that's fifty thousand back to her practice, perhaps over the next year. Let's be conservative so we don't raise any doubts, and say she may only do three of these procedures in a year. Her practice would still make twelve thousand in the first year. Her thirty-two hundred for your weekend seminar yielded her an almost four hundred percent return on investment in year one alone, and now she has that skill to add to the profitability of her practice over the course of her lifetime, while benefiting her patients with this important service. You think she'd be pretty happy about that?"

They looked at me and said, "We never thought about that."

Of course they didn't—they're doctors. Their professional mind-set is about giving the best patient care. And that's perfect, because their customers—other doctors—share that same value. So when pitching their seminar's most attractive features, they should first speak to the audience's values: the benefits to their *patients*. Then communicate the second enticement: the financial value to their private practice. The value suddenly appears far *higher* than the $3,200 cost. Lowering the price tag would have devalued it in their eyes. Now in the participants' mind the seminar cost is relatively low, but its content is not devalued.

Then I gave them another way to turn that $3,200 into a bargain-basement price: by including a value-added offer in their sales presentation. They could tell prospective participants, "To give you the greatest chance of success in your practice, it's important that everyone in your office understand the toxicity analysis procedure. So what we're willing to do is, if you register within the next ten days, you can bring a colleague from your office for an additional $250. That's 75 percent off for you, and you can both teach the others at the office how to benefit more of your patients."

It achieved their objective of getting more "butts in the seats," AND it lowered the price for those who split the cost with a colleague, without devaluing their currency (information). If earlier sign-ups complained that they didn't get the same good deal, the doctors extended the value offer to them, too.

The doctors moved from inside a small frame—focus on price versus value—to the much wider frame of relevance to the *buyers'* values. The added benefit for the doctors was that now they even had participants out there selling their seminar, trying to bring others in, *doing their marketing for them*! Whenever you create incentive for people to go out there and sell your company, that's your funnel.

2. Campaign

Campaigning is like packaging yourself. It's a series of communications that gives you or your company a uniquely distinct presence and a local reputation through various creative, consistent means. You can use this strategy as a leader at many levels while building your company.

I met with a young man who had just received his MBA in international business and finance from a good school. He was ready to start his business but complained that he couldn't find any customers. When I asked him what he was doing to generate sales, he said he had set up a website and was blanketing the town with cards and flyers. I thought, *you just got a degree in business and you can't get more creative and strategic than THAT?*

I said, "Dude, what do you do with the flyers you find stuck under your windshield wiper when you get back to your car?"

"Nothing. I wad them up and throw them away without looking at them."

"Exactly," I said. "Not just because you don't know them from Adam, but because *they* don't know *you*. They don't know who they're pitching to, just as you haven't taken the time to know who you're shooting résumés to. It's a shot in the dark and a waste of ammo. If you don't care what you get, then you *deserve* what you get. It's the most impersonal and ineffective way to find an appropriate position. Figure out who they are and what they want, and let them know how you specifically can help them do that. You automatically gain credibility and attention. Even if they can't give you a job, they could give you better leads."

Think about how Apple positions a new product, or how about Branson? What does Sir Richard Branson do when he wants you to know he just launched a new business? He launches a balloon ride or personally pours drinks for passengers on his airline. He makes the connection. Branson even understands the needs of the press to keep their jobs—they need to entertain their readers to sell papers or news blurbs. He uses uniqueness and humor, and it gets him a lot of free ink. He provides value to the press, and they give value in return. Even the name "Virgin" set his business apart, because its impropriety went against British social conventions at the time.

Of course, you don't have to ride a helium balloon across the sea to create buzz. But you see the qualitative difference between that type of approach and simply sticking a tack through a flyer on a coffee shop bulletin board. That *may be* a fine strategy to start with, but don't stop there. Extreme circumstances call for extreme measures.

Instead of telling others what you need from them—a job, their business, more money—show them all the ways you can help them achieve their strategic objectives and values. Don't just try to plug in to the next empty spot. Be strategic. Craft and hone your campaign to create your own opportunities. President Obama was so innovative in using the Internet to campaign for president, he swept the polls and practically swept all the other candidates under the rug.

When I wanted to expand my valuation business, I hired someone to create a database of all the chairs who ran the conferences for the state CPA societies and bar associations around the country. I then created personable and personal letters outlining the types of unique resources I could provide to their members at their upcoming conferences. I also included an article that I wrote and then customized to each different organization, by giving them a free sample of valuable information: "Please feel free to publish it in your monthly magazine if you think it's of value to your membership." I made sure the topic was highly relevant and specialized to the legal or accounting field. That's very different from asking them for help: "Would you please publish this so I can make a little money and get more exposure?" Instead, this gave editors an easy way for *them* to provide valuable content to their customers. Then I issued press releases every time I was out speaking. The content wasn't about me. It was full of helpful information about the conference itself. Within forty-eight hours, the release was number four on Google, with over sixteen thousand views. The net result was that my name and content were all over the Web and in print. I was asked to speak all over the country. And since my market presence started bringing traffic to my website, I offered video clips and business tips in my blog as one more way potential clients could get valuable information and connect with me and what I do.

Target specific companies you'd like to work with. Read their annual reports; understand their deeper needs; check out their past strategies and current mission statement. From all this information, figure out what's most important to them—then seek to give them exactly what they need. Call the people you want to work with, no matter their position. Give content-full presentations, attention-grabbing events, and exciting press releases that don't just give information but that get into their world and relate to them right where they are.

3. Deliver

The service, product, and experience all have to be positive. To stand out, you have to go beyond their expectations. Zappos upgrades its customers to overnight shipping at no extra charge. Beyond awesome delivery of service, you want to give your market a way to recognize the value of what you gave them. Your positioning and campaigning told them *what* you were going to give them and *why* it was important. Now show them what they got. Having a system of validation in place is generative—it generates loyalty and more business. It gives them a concrete way to value you. It creates customer commitment, which cycles back into repeat business. Customer reviews on your website, for example, generate fans who become spokespeople.

You can add value to your customers' experience and to your own people's experience, simply by celebrating successes. In a culture that loves a good debacle or disaster, honoring others is a wonderful tool for sustainability. Valuing staff encourages more good actions and nourishes the company culture. People generally don't leave jobs for lack of opportunity; they leave for lack of appreciation and satisfaction. Give them the path to grow and gain knowledge, and remember, the failure of an employee is on the shoulders of the manager. Giving always gives back.

4. Serve

We all have our favorite restaurant we like to tell our friends about. What makes it your favorite? It's probably a combination of delivery and service: the food, the atmosphere, the competent and attentive staff—and knowing that you'll get the same quality every time. The place may be an undiscovered hole-in-the-wall, but eventually everyone shows up there and raves about it. *What* they provide (delivery) and *how* they provide it (service) makes up for their lack of advertising. Their customers' word of mouth does their positioning and campaigning for them.

Some companies launch well, then belly flop because they put so much money and effort into their campaign and positioning that they fell short of the high expectations they built up in their customers' minds. A company has to deliver reliably, every time, for its business to be sustainable enough to grow. Anyone heard of McDonald's?

The best strategy is to go out and do what you do over and over again, and fail as quickly and as cheaply as you possibly can. Then get up, take the lessons from it, and keep on going. When I opened the karate school, I decided that we would not be just like most other schools, which treated their business as an assembly line for producing black belts. I saw the belts as a way of letting the students see all they had accomplished, yet the belts weren't the main objective even if they did look good on a college résumé. We decided that our school would be more community service than product, more intention driven than process driven. So we set our intention: *karate is the vehicle; caring is the product.* Our staff understood that it was their job to let every person who walked through our doors know beyond any doubt that they were cared for. It was on us to tailor our service to what would help them grow.

One day, a thirteen-year-old boy came in who had had a brain tumor years earlier. As a result, he had limited sight, cognitive ability, and motor skills. We all noticed that he had a habit, when things got hard, of using his disabilities to escape by having an emotional breakdown. Showing no favor and sticking with our intention to be of service, we did what we do with every other student: we pushed him. We would say, "You're capable of much more, and you'll see it. We're not going to let you give up on yourself." His grandmother thought we were cruel for demanding so much from him. Before he left class, he always had to acknowledge (a) what he first thought he could accomplish that day, and (b) what he actually did accomplish. He had to verify and acknowledge his growth each time. Before this, he had spent two unproductive years in another karate school, which ended in frustration for everyone. After a year with us, the parents were moved to tears over how much he had grown in his confidence and abilities, but also in his maturity—he could stick it out when things got tough, and not fall back on excuses. Our business has grown to a whole next level based on our reputation.

Once you start asking better questions in your business, such as *how do we get our customers to grow personally?* you uplift everything and everyone involved.

It's a much more fulfilling place to do business from when you start to see the caring and serving come back to you.

Show you care. Let your customers and colleagues feel human, because they are. Everyone has different needs. Come from a place of genuine gratitude that you can be of service. And remember, if not for your employees and customers, you wouldn't exist. Your servant leadership mind-set will translate into sustainable growth, because your next happy customer just may be the one who goes out and does your campaigning and positioning for you.

> To access free training and more resources go to:
> **www.theentrepreneurssolution.com/resources**

Fulfill Your Potential and Make a Positive Difference

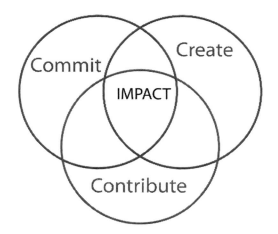

At this stage, you are ready to move your company outward into the world, on whatever scale you wish. The greater your ability to influence others, the broader and deeper your impact can be. This will be done through the understanding of the last three essentials and their respective building blocks of **commit** (mastery and consistency), **contribute** (purpose and growth) and **create** (flexibility and versatility).

CHAPTER 15

COMMIT

Mastery: The Core Commitments of Champions — Life and Business in Balance

Committable Core Values. The key word is "committable":
you must be willing to hire and fire for them.
—Tony Hsieh

COMMITMENT = Consistency + Mastery

A commitment presumes that you are in the game no matter what. It's your commitment to yourself to persevere, and to others that you keep your word. From that consistency, you gain credibility, power, and leverage. It's your commitment to your core values that gives force to your actions.

The day I had my bicycle accident, I was lying facedown and unconscious on the concrete alongside a relatively busy road for I don't know how long before someone stopped—a nurse named Mindy. Paramedics told me later that she called 911 and stayed with me until they came. I don't know who she is or how to find her. I wish I could call her to say thank you, because I know she could easily have chosen *not* to stop, for any number of reasons. She could have been in a hurry or figured someone else would stop. And after all, it was my problem, not hers. I don't know whether she debated with herself whether to stop when she saw me lying there that morning. I do know that my life—if indeed I still had one—would be very different today if she had not been committed to her core values. It was important to her on some level, and as a result, she had an enormous effect on my and my family's life.

The point?

Never underestimate the impact your actions can have. By the same token, think about the ramifications of your *in*actions. If you *don't* start this company, *don't* develop that product, *don't* hire those great people, you rob yourself of opportunities, and others of possibilities. When you build your business, the ripple effect is endless. Suddenly, those you enrolled in your dream now have a new purpose and synergy in their lives. Your product or service is benefiting customers in ways you don't even know. And perhaps your innovative business model inspires other companies to follow suit, as Blake Mycoskie's "one for one" model did.

How Do You Define Success?

Gary Erickson defines success by how he affects others: "The material things we have are not a symbol of success. When someone walks in our door and spends a few hours at Clif Bar and walks out going, 'Wow! That was different,' or when I'm skiing and someone in the chairlift next to me goes, 'Oh, my God, I eat Clif Bars all the time!' that's it right there."

It's the response to your company that becomes your inspiration. Doing good is not an issue of morality or ethics. It's your *nature*. When you tap into this deeper desire to do good in the world, that opens doors, makes connections, sparks collaborations. Be aware of the power you already possess to influence others. Make it your conscious intention to use that power; then watch what happens.

Lying in the ambulance after Mindy left, I certainly wasn't thinking, "I wish I had stuffed more dollars in my pocket." What kept going through my head was, "How could I have done more? Did I really have a positive impact?" In the end, that will be what matters.

Craft your company and product with your impact in mind. Commit to making a difference. You don't have to do it to "help others." You can do it because it makes you feel good, which keeps you highly motivated. Think about it.

Commitment to the Process

Success requires your commitment to the process. And it is a process of trial and error. Your commitment to learning as you go will get you through your company's awkward growth spurts, lending you the strength and tenacity to keep going. I love Nido Qubein's description of this as "faithful courage":

Entrepreneurs are people who are not afraid of failure. They make a distinction between productive failures and nonproductive successes. So when they fail, they dissect the failure; they learn from it so they don't repeat the same mistakes. At the same time, when they succeed they're not quick to just celebrate that. They want to learn from it so they can do it again and again. They have both faith and courage. I like to call it faithful courage. And they have a sense of balance in life that most people do not readily see.

Being an entrepreneur is a multiple-choice test—every day you have multiple choices to make. The difference is that in business, there are no "right" or "wrong" answers. Just results. You either don't like the results, in which case you can improve on them, or you like the results—in which case you can improve on them. Either way, you win. Even if one company "fails," you start the next with new knowledge. One of the greatest benefits of being an entrepreneur is the thrill of overcoming. A champion wins because he or she is not willing to give up.

How Do You Show Up When Challenged?

There are two positions from which to approach life's challenges: offense and defense. Recently we have had perfect illustrations of both playing themselves out in history. The BP oil spill in the Gulf off the Louisiana coastline has been a source of intense conflict. Immediately after the well started spewing millions of gallons of crude oil into the environment, the nation's attention turned to *who* was at fault for the disaster. We didn't get to see everyone involved pull together to ask, *what can we do?* This was no Apollo 13 team at work. Instead, the various companies involved in securing the drill rig began pointing the finger at each other, like kids on a playground. Time was wasted and natural resources and lives destroyed while an epic battle for who was at fault unfolded. The government was blamed for not acting quickly enough to ensure that BP was doing all it could. Local and state authorities wanted to act but waited on authorization. With everyone on the defensive, there was no chance of scoring a big win for everyone concerned.

Compare that response to the collapse of a copper mine in Chile, which trapped thirty-three miners half a mile beneath the earth's surface for months. If you ever wondered what humanity can do with a collaborative entrepreneurial mind, just watch one of the videos of the rescue efforts. The Chilean government committed to rescuing every single miner, without knowing how to accomplish it or whether the miners were even still alive. They did not make their commitment contingent on cost, time, or manpower. Other countries and companies lent help, materials, and money to drill the escape route and innovate a rescue capsule. While the miners themselves had the most to lose, they were the ones to inspire the rest of the world as they pulled together and made their own collaborative effort to stay mentally, emotionally, physically, and even spiritually healthy together during their extreme isolation.

To access free training and more resources go to:
www.theentrepreneurssolution.com/resources

CHAPTER 16

CONSISTENCY: MASTERY—IT'S A PRACTICE, NOT A PINNACLE

COMMITMENT = Consistency + Mastery

It takes years to become an overnight success.
—Eddie Cantor

Bamboo lies dormant under the ground for at least three years. But once it breaks through the ground, you have a full-grown grove of lush bamboo within sixty to ninety days, whether you want it or not. This can be your business's growth pattern, too. With consistency, persistence, and patience, your company can break through the surface of market consciousness and grow like crazy as far as you want to go. As you master each of the Six Stages of Sustainable Success, the company cannot but expand.

Mastery is not the pinnacle of achievement. It is a process that requires practice. As you gain mastery, you will feel balance in life and work, profit and passion, family and business, and everything you are committed to.

The Six Stages of Sustainable Success

These are standard stages of personal growth that we all go through as we progress from complete unawareness that we lack a needed skill, right up through to expert proficiency. I have applied each stage here to the business world to teach entrepreneurs how to move through the same stages, from utter ignorance of what they aren't doing right, to mastery at the top of their field. As you read through the stages, think of what skills you need to improve. They are actually cycles that you will repeat on several levels, in several areas of your business at once, as you work your way to mastery:

First Stage of Sustainable Success: Clueless

One reason why so many entrepreneurs fail the first time around is that they don't know that they don't know. They are *unconsciously* incompetent. They are unaware of what it takes to build a business successfully. Then they read this book, for example. Only then do they realize how much they have yet to learn. Now they are *awakened* incompetent. There is nothing wrong with this stage of growth. In fact, running your own business is the best way to learn. Some of the most successful entrepreneurs started their first business as kids and got their education when they had little to lose. It's unfortunate only when they give up too soon, deciding that they are incompetent. But incompetence is not a permanent condition! It's a temporary phase of growth. Infants are unconsciously incompetent, but not for long. They persist and eventually get on their feet. The key to transitioning out of this phase is to be open to new learnings.

A lot has been said these days about the "necessity entrepreneur." These are the people who find themselves in such a tight financial spot that they quickly launch themselves into a new business without thinking through their plan, if they even have one. I continue to come across stories of first-timers like the guy who engineered a jellyfish tank and threw it on the market before realizing that no one knew how to get hold of a jellyfish. To make his product viable, he had to scramble to find a jellyfish wholesaler online. Then there were the folks who invested their last twenty thousand dollars opening a bakery in the same neighborhood where a bakery just went out of business. When you start your own company, remaining unconscious is not an option. Research your competition, observe how those businesses operate, and seek out experts in your field to act as guides and mentors every step of the way. They will recognize your blind spots and areas where you are sabotaging your success, and remedy the patterns right away.

Second Stage of Sustainable Success: Awakened

At least when you are clueless you were blissfully unaware of your shortcomings. Ideally, at some point, they become glaringly obvious. And that's progress! You are now starkly aware of what you have to learn next. During this phase though most of your results are poor until you are able to shift beyond this phase.

I remember once stepping out onto the mat during a martial arts competition. I had only just mastered the last belt level and was now facing a new opponent. One punch to the solar plexus, and I was down, unable to breathe. It was the beginning of a new learning curve for me. Life constantly challenges us to take on even more skills. In our relationships, our decision-making, our big-picture thinking, our money management, we gain greater and greater competence only to be faced with the next stage of growth. Rather than assume that these are setbacks, see them as stages of artistry.

Here's another demonstration of the mastery cycle. Recently, a family came to me for some consulting work after the mother passed away. When their father had passed away five years earlier, they were worth $180 million. By the time the sons and daughter came for help, they were worth $5 million and sinking fast, with no idea why. Had they simply put that $180 million in the bank earning 5 percent (at the time), it would have earned them $750,000 per month—an easy enough sum to live on for a month even if it's split four ways. The problem in this case—and that I see in many cases—was that the parents passed on wealth without ever considering the importance of passing on the *skills* needed to manage and grow that wealth. It's a true reflection of what happened in our larger economy. This family's dire circumstances became a jumping-off point for them to gain conscious competence in managing their own money and learning the mechanics of their business. And they were highly motivated. My job, then, became less about simply reallocating funds and more about retraining their mind-set and teaching them the Business Mastery Blueprint™ so they could gain mastery over their own destiny.

During this awakening phase, it is only through taking action on what is presenting itself to you that you can transition beyond it to the next phase of Deliberate.

Third Stage of Sustainable Success: Deliberate

Back in the early nineties, I was trying to build my clientele within a firm. No attorney wanted to hire me because, they said, "You've got no testimony experience." I was conscious of my incompetence in that specific area. It was a catch-22, though: I wanted to gain the experience testifying in front of a court, yet no one would give me the chance, because I had no experience. *How do you gain competence in a new area without risking your business?* The specific answer to that question will be different for every business, but the bottom line is always the same: *do it!*

I figured that if I started speaking in front of groups, it would teach me to articulate and answer questions on the fly. As in chess, I was putting myself in position to make a lateral move later. Well, what I didn't realize then but do now is that going out there to practice speaking also created visibility. And that visibility created credibility, which generated profit from several directions. The choice to become competent in a new area was a stretch. It also turned out to be a risk that would change my future forever. It was so important to me to continue expanding my skills that I took that opportunity in 1997 to speak at the conference in Arkansas—and that decision finally caused the firm I was working with to let me go. As it turned out, being "let go" freed me to pursue my passions. I have had at least one job in Arkansas every single year but one since 1997. Scary though it was at the time, this marked the end of my partnership, and the beginning of a flourishing career.

So as I stepped out on the speaking platform, I made no false claims and made it my job to convey the perception of credibility. Though I lacked experience, what I did have in spades was desire, drive, and the education to back it. The more I spoke, the more my audiences thought, *he's been around—he must be good.* What started as a perception created the positioning. From that practice came conscious competence. So that is a great example of what I mean when I say that the *mind-set*—my willingness to stretch my self-perception and learn a new skill—created part of the *marketing*, which grew the *mechanics* of the business and expanded the *money* sources.

Through this deliberate action you will find yourself making more progress although your results may still be only mediocre until through a diligent repetition of effort you truly cross what I call the "money line" to the next phase where things begin to Flow.

You Have to Believe in You Before Others Can.
Our degree of happiness and motivation lies in how we frame events in the mind. We tend to focus on the things we see as lack, and disregard all that is good. If we label something or someone "bad," we assume we can't do anything about it. This makes us unhappy, which makes everything else start to look bad and out of our control, including ourselves. So it's important that we speak about what we're grateful for and what is good in our lives.

Give credit where credit is due. In business, when your progress slows or you lose direction, become conscious of your competence—acknowledge yourself and those on your team for how far you've come. Take in the view. Notice what is working well. Do a personal inventory of your strengths, and recognize the lessons indicating what you need to change. A little self-congratulation goes a long way. It brings more joy to the journey, and fuel for the next phase of your growth.

Fourth Stage of Sustainable Success: Flowing
Consistent practice ingrains habits in our unconscious mind until they become automatic. When you are doing your job so well that someone says, "It's like you can do it in your sleep," they are talking about your unconscious competence. You can complete certain complex tasks, such as brushing your hair or backing out of the driveway, because you've "done it a million times." The singular focus

and repetition creates a set pattern of doing something well. Through the dogged pursuit of their dreams, artists and athletes develop sensory attunements and muscle memory, and successful CEOs develop a leadership style that works even in the midst of cataclysmic changes.

This type of repetitive work will allow you to better your results beyond mediocre to good yet when you decide to shift your mind-set to a place of wanting to be one of the best – a master. This is where you will begin to find the true achievements and successes you dream and read about.

Fifth Stage of Sustainable Success: Mastery

Reading the market, making judgment calls, communicating with your team—eventually, it all feels instinctive. Beyond just memorizing the mechanics, you understand the principles. Success isn't a formulaic equation. It's taking your knowledge to a deeper level so you can extrapolate any situation. We all have seen masters such as Michael Jordan, who can change direction in the same moment his brain has the thought to move, who can focus and shoot and consistently score win after win. This is mastery. You play life as a game. Choose your next move. Arrive at your own definition of success. Decide to be the best at what you do, and go for it. This is living a life that matters.

Rise to Your Own Standard of Excellence.

You may be very competent according to the achievement standards of others, but striving to reach *your own* standard will take you even higher. Play by your own rules and standards. You can't master every skill. Choose to pursue what is meaningful and fun for you.

Be internally compelled. It will put you in a whole other realm than if you were driven by perks, dangling carrots, or retirement years. Master your mental and emotional states. Masterful CEOs have self-mastery. They have an edge because they live life on their own terms.

There is an idea that matters to you, a talent you have and want to hone, a desire to excel in something. *What brings you so much satisfaction that you want to sink all your energy into it?*

Decide

I said that to gain conscious competence, you have to acknowledge your strengths so you can build on them. Now you need to acknowledge your limitations, because mastery lies in your decision to overcome them.

In 1997, I herniated three disks in my back at the karate studio because I was throwing students without having warmed up properly. I couldn't walk, and lying in bed offered little relief from the pain that ran down to my toes. An orthopedic surgeon recommended surgery to cut away the disks. The endgame of his plan was that I would eventually end up with several fused vertebrae— effectively like having a steel rod in my back.

I said, "I'm not going to allow that to happen to me."

He said, "That's your only choice unless you want to live with this pain getting worse."

I thanked him and walked out. That was his belief system, I told myself. Not mine.

The pain persisted for months, during which I tried alternative treatments, yet I was often tempted just to have it go away under the knife. A friend who had watched me suffer for months encouraged me to get the operation. One day as I was laid up in bed, I actually called to make the surgery appointment. But the thought persisted: *I'll only be replacing my temporary pain with the terminal pain of regret.* I remember getting off the phone and saying, "I never quit before—why am I willing to quit now?"

I canceled the surgery appointment and spoke with the doctor instead. I said, "We've got to dig deeper. I'm not quitting. Just tell me what I've got to do, and I'll do it."

Knowing me well, my doctor said, "Okay, you need to manage the pain— and your patience."

That was the moment I felt my body start to heal. I decided. I knew what I had to do. It was a done deal. I didn't have any choice but to get better. The shift came when I took responsibility. I was not consciously aware that I had been on the fence for years, unsure whom to believe: myself or the doctors. Then suddenly, the moment I aligned with my own truth, it was as if my back began its own realignment. I committed to doing whatever it took, but I drew the line at surgery. We combined epidural injections with acupuncture, traction, physical therapy, and massage, and I'm on the other side of it now.

The moment you make the decision, you eliminate all other possibilities. That's when options open up that you didn't see before.

Teach What You Know.

When I chose to specialize in the valuation field, I didn't want just to read every court case that pertained to valuation, and pass the certification test. It would have been enough according to industry standards, but I wanted to master the subject according to my own standards. So I approached my learning it as if I had to teach it to others. I knew that if I approached the material as if I had to present it, I would understand it that much better. As a result, I got it at a much deeper level. And within the next few years, I actually began to teach it! As I spoke about valuation from the stage, I began to receive requests to testify in cases for companies and law firms, the IRS, the Department of Justice, and the Department of Labor. Then, because of all the consulting work I was doing, I was asked to be on various boards of directors. My commitment to my strategy had paid off.

When you study a subject as if you had to teach it, you store it differently in your mind. You make your own sense of it. Rather than just be able to regurgitate it, you make it your own, which creates your reputation.

Sixth Stage of Sustainable Success: Artistry

Mastery is still not the peak. You don't arrive at a point of mastery and stop. It's yet another opening—to *artistry*.

Artistry is taking the gifts and talents that you have mastered and bringing them into a much larger realm, where you can have a global impact. It's the rarified air of inspiration, where you hear a higher calling and are willing to answer when destiny calls. You're so artfully competent at this stage, you could choose to change the world if you wanted to. This is a place where you have found the joy in what you do for the sake of doing it. It is through this search and embracing of joy that you will find your epic journey into artistry. Artistry is really the subject of the next four chapters, as your life's work becomes about what you can now *create* and *contribute*.

> To access free training and more resources go to:
> **www.theentrepreneurssolution.com/resources**

CHAPTER 17

FLEXIBILITY: LIFE AND BUSINESS IN THE BALANCE

CREATIVITY = Flexibility + Versatility

Prepare yourself for the world as the athletes do for their exercise. Oil your mind and your manners, to give them the necessary suppleness and flexibility. Strength alone won't do.
—**Lord Chesterfield**

Many years back, when rental cars and cell phones didn't have GPS, I had an important business meeting scheduled in Dallas. After landing at the airport, I headed out into the city in my rental car, feeling pretty confident with my most modern of advantages: MapQuest directions, printed out on the passenger seat beside me—until I was hit with the unexpected. Barely out of the airport, I ran into road construction and a sign that said, "DETOUR." That was it. I came undone. My MapQuest directions stopped being relevant. I started going left, right, left, and quickly lost all perspective. I hadn't anticipated any problems, so I had no alternative routes planned. I had no phone number for the meeting place to tell them I'd be late, no contact person to ask for directions. Dallas is a sprawling city, so the farther off course I sensed I was getting, the more my emotions were on the rise, competing with my rational thinking for headspace. It was a disaster of my own making. Could I blame MapQuest for not foreseeing the construction detour? Why not? Everybody does. But the smarter solution would have been to expect roadblocks and come prepared.

How to Prevent Disaster (or Handle It When You Haven't)

You can get where you want to go from wherever you are at. Anticipate detours and have alternate routes to reach your objective. That's flexibility: the ability to stretch and stay fluid in your thinking, to see your plan from several points of view, and to listen to your intuition and act in the moment when it is relevant and necessary.

When Zappos was only a few months away from closing its doors due to lack of profitability and cash flow, Tony Hsieh was sure he had exhausted all his options. On the verge of saying good-bye to his beautiful idea one afternoon while having a drink with a colleague, Tony asked a simple question: "What if we shipped directly out of our own warehouse?" He and his team had been using a drop-ship model that they had never even questioned up to that point. Doing the numbers, they saw that this new little strategy could potentially triple their sales. Suddenly, a glimmer of a light appeared at the end of the tunnel. It did much more than triple Zappos' sales. It eventually skyrocketed the company into a position where it had a deal value of $1.2 billion to Amazon.

Flexibility is not just reactive; it's proactive. Here are several ways you can develop this essential entrepreneurial asset to prevent disasters and create something amazing with the raw materials in your mind:

1. Generate Options; Ask, *What if . . .*

Airline pilots are alerted to turbulence in their path before they get there, so they can choose to fly above, below, around, or through the rough patch. To avert a crisis, it helps to have options before you need them. As you initiate a project or launch, you want to ask, *what problems can I anticipate? What strategies or directions would help me sidestep them?* Brainstorm any and every path that will get you there. Strategic flexibility is using whatever ethical option is open to you.

As a business strategist, it doesn't matter whether I'm working with corporations or first-time start-ups—I always tell them the same thing: first, give me your strategic business plan. They sit down and spend days or weeks working out an airtight plan. Then we go through it together, and I say, "That's great. Now, put that aside and give me a *new* business plan.

They always ask, "What's wrong with the last one?"

"Nothing's wrong with it," I reply. "I still want another one."

They go back to the drawing board and bring me another plan. The second is often more creative than the first, because they have had to think through the same issues in a different way. They proudly hand me their second business plan, and I say, "Great! Now give me another plan."

After they get over their initial frustration, they go away for a while and come back with a third plan. Their end goal, financial projections, and dream are all still there on the page, but now they have had to dig a lot deeper and account for contingencies. After the fifth or sixth time, they finally wonder aloud, "Are you out of your freaking mind?"

This is when I let them know, "No, I'm not; however, I am trying to put you out of *your* mind. Success is not an entirely logical process. It's ultimately intuitive and creative. The one thing you *can* predict is this: Your business is not going to unfold in the way you planned it. It can still go smoothly if you have so many alternative routes lined up that you can maneuver quickly and instinctively around or through anything that comes up. Even if you can't anticipate market changes, now you've seen your business from every angle. You know what you're capable of, so you won't have to panic. You'll just have to adapt. Writing a business plan isn't about getting it right the first time and setting it in stone. It's an exercise in thinking and rethinking until you know you can respond creatively to any circumstance."

Have a Plan B, C, D, and right through to Z if it makes you feel indomitable. Don't get so fixated on one particular path that you fail to see alternatives. Keep your eye on that ultimate destination, and be willing to take whatever path gets you there.

2. Approach Outside Changes With Humility and Eager Anticipation

One day an older-looking gentleman walked into our karate studio. I assumed he was there to sign up a grandchild, so I led him into my office. The moment we sat down, he said, "Listen, I had a stroke two years ago and I recovered. Then last year, I lost my wife of fifty-five years, and I can't say I'm recovered from that, but I figured something out."

"Okay," I said, not knowing where he was going with this.

"I can either sit back and wait until God decides to take me back so I can be with my wife again, or I can come in here and do something that I always wanted to do all my life. Do you take seventy-four-year-old students?"

I was thrilled. I said, "Absolutely!"

"I have some limitations."

I said, "We all have limitations. We work with them and get over them or we work around them. You can be our inspiration." He trained with us for two years before moving away, but he continues to be an example for my team and me.

Be willing to learn and grow your whole life. Some of the biggest, stoutest trees are the ones most susceptible to getting toppled in a storm. Why? Because they are so rigid. It's the tree that bends with the changing winds that weathers the storms.

As an entrepreneur, you will be required at some point to demonstrate flexibility in the face of outside forces: new market preferences, global economic shifts, changing laws, health-care bills, fresh competition, technological advancements, environmental changes, and terrorism, to name but a few. Businesses are buffeted constantly by outside forces. You can look for the advantage or disadvantage in each. I recommend that you seek the advantage. It's better to *over*estimate their potential effect on your business than to underestimate it. The companies that thought blogging and Facebook were play toys and that didn't see China coming are scrambling now while others enjoy the benefits of having an online presence and a global strategy. Look for the relevant wave of opportunity and take advantage of it early. Keep an open mind at every age and every stage of your company's growth.

3. Navigate and Adapt to Inner Change

It's obvious that we have to ride the swells of cultural progress happening around us. It's not as obvious that we need to stay aware of internal shifts in our priorities. Change can seem to come overnight, as when a marriage ends, a business fails, or a shoelace gets caught in a bike chain. Or it can come glacially over time. In all cases, changes serve as a reminder to keep pace with what is meaningful to *you*.

When Tony Hsieh still headed up his first business, LinkExchange, he reluctantly had to admit to himself at some point that it had stopped being as fun when it grew so big he didn't know all his employees anymore. His profits were still climbing, but his happiness quotient was dropping. He added his happiness and well-being into the success equation, didn't like the way it penciled out, and decided to sell the business.

Many people believe that it's better to be "rich and unhappy" than "poor and happy," because they figure that once you're rich, you can *make* yourself happy. But most discover, after sacrificing their heart on the altar of false security for so long, that it's hard to get that joy back. Hsieh saw another alternative: instead of being "rich and unhappy," he could be "richer and happier."

At every stage of your business, you can make new choices that are aligned with your deeper desires. Let your company's growth keep pace with your inner growth. Continue asking yourself, *am I on the path with my passion and purpose?* As you grow and innovate, your success should always come full circle back to your personal *identity, ideals,* and *intentions.* Your "Three I's" are never set in stone. Just keep your finger on the pulse of your own heart at all times. It will tell you what direction to take next. The more you make your decisions this way on the small stuff, the more you will trust your wisdom on the big executive decisions.

4. Seek Out Change and Growth

You wouldn't think that finally attaining a measure of success could ever pose a problem. After all, that's when you finally got what you wanted! You arrived!

Well, if you think fear of failure is rough, try its lesser-known sidekick: *fear of success.* I've seen entrepreneurs freeze up at the height of success, as if they had a fear of those heights, because now they're afraid of losing it all. They get it in their heads, *now we have further to fall. Everyone is expecting only great things now; I can't disappoint them.* All entrepreneurs feel the responsibility of their employees who rely on them, but these successful entrepreneurs start to second-guess themselves. They are often unaware that their fear has started to change their decision-making style. Either they feel justified now in "doing everything the way it's always been done, because that's what works," or they shift to risk-aversion strategies. Their loss of flexibility is insidious. They stop seeking out change and growth.

Kodak got left behind for some years when cameras went digital. The company had been at the top of the game for so long, its presumption that the top was its natural position eventually threatened its sustainability. Kodak didn't see the digital wave as a game changer that would make film basically irrelevant. Polaroid got hammered for the same reason: complacency born of overconfidence.

There are a million and one things that can get you off your game, even when you're at the top. Don't get complacent just because you've reached your goals. While "the game" will always change, the rules never do—keep employing the creative thinking that gets you your success.

5. Learn From Your Mistakes

Have you ever noticed how many studies of disasters show that they could have been prevented if only warnings had been heeded or protocol were followed? After the devastating tsunami in 2004 killed at least two hundred thousand people in several East Asian countries, local organizations under UNESCO set about improving the early-warning system that had existed for forty years. But competition among countries to host the system's headquarters slowed the process. Their plan to improve communications across continents collapsed as various nations balked at sharing data and responsibility and fought over their share of profits. Two years later, in 2006, another tsunami struck the same region, and seven hundred died for the same reason: communications were still not in place to get early warnings to those to whom that information mattered most. Hence another unfortunate example of when collaboration would have been more productive than competition.

The moment we open our entrepreneurial minds to the possibility that prosperity need not be predicated on others' loss and suffering or require that most of the world live in poverty—that is the moment we can create new ways. I'm sure that some great success stories will come out of this era, because we've got our backs up against a wall. The trick is this: think of being creative and flexible, not as a luxury but as if your life depended on it—because it does.

6. Value Yourself; Find Balance in the Process

I had a client once who spent a good chunk of money with the firm every year and, every year, was a source of chronic aggravation to my employees and me. Without fail, when he got our bill he would call me and try to negotiate it down. It was such a hassle that one year I told him, "The money you pay me isn't enough."

He got irate: "What do you mean? You want *more*?"

I said, "No. We do this every year. I made an extra ten grand, but in the process I got yelled at and cussed out. You may get away with your anger at home, and you may get away with it with your own employees, but I'm not going to ask my people to go through this lack of appreciation or respect again. If you don't value the work I do as much as *I* value it, find someone else. Pay them what you want, and don't ever call me again."

He sent me the whole amount with an apology and wanted to work with me again. I said no thank you and never picked him up again. My peace of mind and my employees' appreciation were worth far more than his check. And better clients came in to fill the void.

Once I got to the point in my career that it was more important for me to make a life than to make a living, I was no longer willing to accept less than the value I gave.

Get a vision for the types of clients and customers you want; then hold on to that ideal. When you value yourself more, your company's value automatically goes higher, too. Communicate your standards ahead of time. Tell others exactly what you are willing to do and what you are not willing to do. If someone professes not to understand your needs and requirements, they are probably not the most desirable client to have anyway. Drop detrimental clients before you ever drop your own standards. Personal power is your ability to say no and go on enjoying the process.

Many budding entrepreneurs wonder, *how can I manage a business and a family or relationship at the same time?* This is how. It comes back to managing your focus. When you clearly know your priorities, you can put the phone down or stop checking e-mails at all hours of the night, so that your time with family is uninterrupted. You have to ask yourself, *when is enough, enough?* Predetermine your standards up front, as you start the business, so that you know when you have fulfilled them. You can always choose new standards.

Apply the same ideals to your professional career that you have in your personal life, so you no longer have to live a dichotomy of work and life. Don't put off fulfillment for the future. Fulfillment is a product of balance in your life. Know what you are willing to sacrifice, and what you are not. This is how you balance the scales.

To access free training and more resources go to:
www.theentrepreneurssolution.com/resources

CHAPTER 18

VERSATILITY: ENTREPRENEURS AS ARTISTS

CREATIVITY = Flexibility + Versatility

Leadership is primarily a high-powered right brain activity. It's more of an art; it's based on a philosophy. You have to ask the ultimate questions of life—once you have resolved them, you have to manage yourself effectively to create a life congruent with your answers.
—Stephen R. Covey

W e tend to think of entrepreneurs as being the almost diametrical opposites of artists. One seems to represent power, wealth, and stability while the other evokes images of free-thinking, pushing-the-envelope expression and living on the edge. The truth is, an entrepreneur needs the artist's traits as much as the artist needs the CEO's. And the most successful CEOs demonstrate a strong balance of both.

If you see yourself primarily as an artist, this entrepreneurial essential will come easily to you for several reasons:

- You naturally see potential where others don't.
- You love to dream up new applications for old ideas.
- You bring a visionary quality to your business model.
- You enlist and inspire those around you to think big and bold.
- You use your special talents to make your business stand out from the rest.

If you consider yourself more of an entrepreneur type and believe that you lack creativity, then you can learn some new skills:

- Develop your right-brain thinking to lead your team.
- Create integrative solutions.
- Envision possible future opportunities.
- Imagine how your company can be a leader in your industry.
- Recognize creative minds, and hire them when and where you need them.

Be the Game Changer

For a moment let's put some of Tiger Woods's recent personal choices aside and look at his golf game only. Even though Tiger Woods was at the top of his game, exceeding everyone else's standards and expectations, he decided to reinvent his swing. In the process, his game hit a slump. But the pro knew that it would be temporary and worthwhile. He envisioned a perfect swing, and he set about creating it as he saw it. Then, just when we all thought it couldn't possibly improve, his game got that much better.

Woods has changed the game of golf by constantly holding himself up to higher and higher standards of his own making (it is unfortunate he didn't do this in his personal life too). To take a skill that you have already mastered over your whole lifetime and retrain your mind and body to do it differently—and better—is nothing short of awesome. That is what I call artistry. Woods wasn't content with doing it just one way. He wanted to build versatility into his game. That requires the ultimate flexibility in mind-set and motor coordination. He didn't settle for being the best; something within him insisted on constant growth. It's the entrepreneurial mind's desire to reach for the highest potential. Each of us has it. The only thing that holds us back is our unwillingness to change our ways.

Versatility—the ability to easily change course—has been an underrated skill in the business world because it was often mistaken for being wishy-washy, indecisive, noncommittal. Now the ability to change course at the drop of a hat is a necessity. Change is inevitable. Progress is intentional.

Companies that can turn on a dime do so because they take the initiative. They don't just adapt to the changes happening all around them. They create change—in their market, in their strategies, in their company culture, and in the world at large.

You Know You're an Artist when . . .

You know you're an artist when you lend your perspective to a project or problem, and people say, "Hmm . . . I never thought of it that way before." You create your life in your own image. You get an inspired vision and follow it through to fruition. You see unnecessarily problematic areas and feel compelled to design a better way for them to work. You see the common causes that connect people beneath their differences. You have the boldness to set projects in motion "before their time," because bigger ideas inspire you. You insist on change, even if it means learning new skills, because you actually enjoy challenging yourself. You lead with your heart and use whatever is in play at the moment. You look at possibilities from several viewpoints to synthesize various elements, people, and disciplines. And whatever you do, you like to master it and move on. Whether you are working in someone else's company or your own, you make your work your own because you are an artist at heart, designing your life the way you want it.

Expand Exponentially

Can we foresee unpredictable changes in the market? No, but we can build flexibility and versatility—in business terms, scalability and expandability—into our product and service designs, and even into our business model. Too often when a business arrives at the critical point where it needs to expand or die, entrepreneurs mistakenly think that taking on a partner for a cash infusion is their best (or perhaps only) option. But there are many other progressive ways to accomplish growth that don't involve the financial risks of taking on a partner, selling out, or merging.

Here are just a few ways to apply a versatility model to expand your business's profit base:

1. Collaborative Business Ventures (Not Traditional Partnerships)

Apple's willingness to let go of 100 percent control of its product and make its apps platform available to outside sources has made the iPhone a money machine. Even Apple didn't know that it would average $1 million a day in that first month, then a billion downloads less than a year later, and, as of this writing, more than seven billion. This represents a new kind of ever-expanding, collaborative business model in which "partners" don't own a percentage of the company itself. If Apple is unhappy with an app's performance or content, it can simply remove it, making it far less risky than some traditional partnerships, where owners are forced to buy out their partners' stake and can lose millions of dollars in the process.

When you think innovatively about how your company could benefit from collaborative relationships, always think in terms of win-wins. Beyond the simple company-to-customer relationship, think up new models of benefit. Be as creative as you want, and propose your ideas to others who could profit right along with you. If someone came to you with some new ways to expand your business with their help, wouldn't you listen? You have nothing to lose and everything to gain.

2. Build Scalability into Your Plan

Here are two great examples of expansion through versatility—again, Apple and Amazon. Apple decided to imagine a future in which it was still viable, and came up with the Apple Pro Tower. It's designed for future modifications so that it doesn't ever have to slip into obsolescence. Rather than build them like the old refrigerators that were timed to stop working after a few years, thus forcing consumers to consume, Apple built the product so we can hold on to the hardware and continue upgrading its software. That's smart scalability, and a brilliant demonstration of planned sustainability instead of planned obsolescence—for the environment and the bottom line. The company won't have the expense of manufacturing new hardware, and we won't pay the price in environmental toxins and landfill capacity due to discarded hardware.

Amazon also has one eye on the realities of today, and the other on the future. After building mastery and a quality reputation in one area—books— it lifted its entire operation up to the next plateau to become the new Sears, delivering almost everything we need, right to our doorstep. What else could a company ask for? Answer: a larger profit margin, as it turns out. And how could the largest online retailer possibly expand further? Answer: headfirst into virtual space. Since 2007, Amazon has been expanding into the Elastic Compute Cloud, or "EC2." EC2 is a Web service that provides resizable compute capacity in the cloud. It is designed to make Web-scale computing easier for developers.

Why the shift from a focus on retail for consumers to service for corporations? After Amazon compared its profit margin from e-commerce (less than 2 percent) with Google's (around 29 percent), it became obvious that Amazon had something more valuable than well-priced shoes or even iPods: its own database. Every time we make a purchase or do a search on Amazon, the company collects and owns the data that represents our buying habits and interests and product preferences. Corporate finally got creative and decided to reach for the clouds! Its new business model allows it to get out from under all those shipping costs and finally put to use its real value—which is, of course, all the consumer-based information it has acquired over years of building traffic on its site. Selling information is even more profitable than selling everything else.

Look at your business plan upside down and inside out. *Are the strategies you've been using from the past still serving you today and into the future? Reexamine the data that you have always looked at it, and see it with fresh eyes. Gather the troops and invite them to offer fresh perspectives on the company's latent potential. Think in several directions at once. Start asking open-ended questions:*

3. Solicit Ideas from Others—and *Listen*

John Kennedy made one promise to the American people, and that was that we would walk on the moon "in this decade." And we did. He had no idea how we would get there. He had an objective, not a plan. He demonstrated the open-minded possibility thinking of the greatest leaders. Then he solicited the help of many others to tell him *how* it could be done.

The best leaders solicit others' ideas and input. Clarence Otis, Chairman and CEO of Darden Restaurants, worked his way up from his childhood in Watts during the nineteen-sixties to become one of the only African-American CEOs of a Fortune 500 company. He attributes much of his success to the power of listening:

"You have to allow room for other people to express their views. As you move into leadership positions, if you are quick to express your point of view, you never hear anyone else's. There is a lot to be said about the power of being quiet versus the power of being heard. I had a self-awareness of how I came across to others. That's important. I didn't want to come off as crowding other people out. I don't think any good manager should."

There's a big difference between possibility thinking and lack thinking, and it can make a big difference in your bottom line. To discover your company's versatility, don't just surround yourself with like-minded people who are likely to agree with you all the time. Create some kind of forum where *un*like minds can speak freely. Listening is a great way to let everyone in your company know that you value their input.

4. Value "Right Brain" Thinkers

Curing degenerative diseases is serious business, best left to the best and brightest minds of the scientific community . . . right? Well, not necessarily. When it comes to folding proteins, not even the most cutting-edge computer programs developed to decode the biochemistry behind certain diseases can outperform gamers. A boldly innovative new game called FoldIt (fold.it) gives anyone with an iPhone or Internet access the chance to help find a cure for everything from allergies to neurodegenerative diseases. What we know is that when proteins are improperly folded, one of their natural functions—carrying clear signals from the brain to the body and feeding muscles—is weakened. What we don't know is what the healthiest protein structure looks like. And the numbers of possible configurations are astronomical. So in one act of genius and humility, biologists and computer scientists at the University of Washington sought out the help of others. They developed a game that could take advantage of puzzle solvers' intuitive, compulsive, and competitive nature to predict the structure of a protein. Now they are getting better results, in less time, than if they only employed modern technology. That's because computers are logical and systematic, whereas people are logical and instinctive. So although solving the world's problems was never child's play, now maybe it is.

"Creatives" are more and more valuable in our ever-changing marketplace. But they also need the support of a team and a clear-minded leader to set them in a direction.

A great example of this idea of collaborative creativity is the open-source research and development company InnoCentive. If you haven't heard of it yet, you will. Its tagline is, "InnoCentive harnesses creative brainpower around the world to solve problems that really matter." Now Toyota is asking consumers, "How would you design your ideal car?" Getting new ideas from outside sources and experts in other fields is called *open innovation*. It can eliminate the guessing game and engage customers.

Be as imaginative as you are systematic. Or use the brain trust you have by soliciting ideas from typically right brainoriented departments such as Marketing and Human Resources. They don't need to understand the financials of the business to open your eyes to new solutions you may never have considered. "Right brainers" can form a more integrative, holistic picture.

5. Use Your Talents to Serve a Higher Purpose

Jackie Chan went far beyond mastery of his martial arts discipline, into artistry. Now he uses his skills to develop multiple businesses and nonprofits. He seems to create synergy in all his many new ventures without breaking stride. Like the rest of us, though, Chan started with nothing but unconscious incompetence. Demonstrating the core commitments of a champion, he mastered the moves in martial arts so well that, like a true artist, he then created his own martial arts style. When he took his talents to the movie screen in China, he quickly became one of that country's most beloved stars, and one of ours. Once in America, his character, courage, and charm made it easy for him to connect with other creative minds, and he began directing films and collaborating on creative projects that were more meaningful to him. His megastardom was not an end point but another jumping-off point. His creative approach to life kept him growing.

After launching several of his own businesses, in his pursuit to make a positive difference in the world, he used his renown and wealth to support several sustainability projects: to save tigers, conserve natural resources, help flood victims, prevent animal abuse, promote scientific research, and develop youth through the performing arts. He also serves as a UNICEF goodwill ambassador—a role to which he brings much humor and humility. In other words, Jackie Chan didn't sit back on his celebrity and collect royalty checks. He decided to be a catalyst for change. And that is a choice we need to recognize as heroic and, in our shrinking world, necessary.

I say "necessary" because it represents the versatility to stretch our perception beyond being self-referential, to become *other*-referential, where we see our lives in the context of the whole. Rather than *what can I do to get by today? the question becomes how can I use my talents to make others' lives better?*

Living our work as if it were our life's purpose is not only the most exciting and rewarding place to grow a business from; it is also the most effective, because our business expands right along with our wider vision for our future. We are willing to reach beyond our comfort zone and willing to make mistakes and take criticism. Beyond money and accolades, we, as entrepreneurs, are pulled forward by a higher mandate.

To access free training and more resources go to:
www.theentrepreneurssolution.com/resources

CHAPTER 19

PURPOSE: HIGH-IMPACT BUSINESS — MORE PURPOSE-DRIVEN THAN PROFIT-OBSESSED

Few will have the greatness to bend history itself; but each of us can work to change a small portion of events, and in the total of all those acts will be written the history of this generation.
—**Robert Kennedy**

CONTRIBUTION = Impact + Change

Small Acts Can Create Big Change

Have you ever woken up in a bad mood and encountered a happy person, or maybe a beautiful sunrise, that turned your whole day around? Have you ever noticed the ripple effect your positive mood then had on others? We each have the ability to affect others. What we don't usually know is the degree to which our actions affect others, our social network, and ever-widening circles in society, whether positively or negatively. The metaphor most often used to illustrate this idea of cause and effect is that of a butterfly's wingbeats creating an infinitesimal ripple in the atmosphere, whose effect can then create, delay, accelerate, or prevent a tornado in an entirely different time and place. This is known as the butterfly effect. It was used by environmental scientists to illustrate "sensitive dependence": that a small change that occurs in one place within a complex system with interacting variables can create much larger changes elsewhere.

If a mere butterfly can do all that, imagine how one business initiative can cause a chain of events that eventually leads to large-scale change, for better or for worse: in your company, your family, the economy, the world at large. One man starts a program enabling the townspeople to bring their empty bottles to the local school so they can cash them in to pay for the school's music program. Other schools around the country start using the same idea to generate income for their endangered art programs. Or one big company makes a bad decision on an oil rig, and an entire region loses multiple sources of income as wide swaths of delicate ecosystem are damaged.

There are no closed systems. We all now live in a world that was created by the choices of those who went before us. And every moment of every day, our smallest actions are creating the world where our children will live tomorrow. Before you freak out at that level of responsibility, consider that you are already changing the world every day with your choices. The question, then, is not whether you contribute to the world. Here are the real questions:

- *What do you **want** to contribute to the world?*
- *How do your everyday actions affect others?*
- *What small or big mark would you like to make on the future?*
- *What would you enjoy leaving behind for future generations?*

The New Entrepreneur

The twenty-first century's entrepreneurs will differentiate themselves in history by creating new business models that include social causes in their mission and in their profit structure. It's happening already. It is so obvious that the globe is shrinking that even while divisive politics rage on, there is a growing understanding across continents that "we are all in this together." In the past, our natural environment may have seemed impervious to human influence. Now the cause-and-effect relationship between our choices and our living environment is ever more obvious. Again, there is no such thing as a closed system. Even if you are a small business, you can have a big impact. There is a huge cultural shift happening in our perspective and our priorities.

The collective realization of the overarching interconnectedness of everything introduces marvelous opportunities to innovate new strategies for sustaining profit, people, *and* the planet. That's right, folks: introducing the new triple bottom line! The most progressive companies have been aware for it for least three or four decades. Now others are catching on to the fact that you can't measure one without the other two. That idea alone is gaining momentum and shifting the way we do business. It is these businesses that are truly sustainable over the long term because they will enlist and engage their employees, vendors, and the public with something more meaningful than simply dollars—something that is fulfilling their higher purpose and values.

Right about now you may be thinking, *contribute? Sure, big corporations and billionaires like Bill Gates can make a difference. But I'm just trying to make payroll! I don't have the luxury of thinking of others' needs right now. I've got to think of my family first. And it takes too much time to do community service—time I just don't have!*

Again, the challenge lies in the mind-set. People tend to think either *if I try to help others, there's no money in it*, or *I shouldn't make money by helping people.* Both are based on dichotomous thinking—an erroneous model that's gotten us all into a double bind. Somewhere along the way, we separated the twins "doing well while doing good," put them in opposite corners, and said, "It's impossible to feed both at the same time." That's the old-school way of thinking. If anyone can solve that conundrum, it's an entrepreneur!

When called on to save humanity from itself, some entrepreneurs still say, "It's not my job. I'm just trying to stay afloat." But the new entrepreneur understands that we are already in the trenches together. As individuals, as a nation, and as a global community, we can solve our challenges together or die trying. I have always said, if we have the ability, that makes it our responsibility.

Profit and Philanthropy: A Marriage Made in Heaven

Today's corporate initiatives may very well be more marketing than altruism. That doesn't lessen the difference that their contributions make. Making one's contributions known has always made good marketing sense. It also inspires others to do the same.

PepsiCo likes to set up public challenges such as the Crash the Super Bowl contest, in which anyone can create and submit a thirty-second commercial to play during the Super Bowl, then win up to a million bucks if viewers vote their piece the best. The company spent a hefty chunk of its airtime and marketing funds on the challenge, knowing that it would engage viewers enough to drive traffic to the online site to vote. It did—the challenge got a better voter turnout than the last presidential election.

PepsiCo has extended its reach even further into the online world by having challenges for charitable organizations to win up to $250,000 and for young, risk-taking social media start-ups to pitch their most innovative ideas to change the world. The money the company saves on high-priced advertising campaigns goes toward all kinds of other causes, such as its Entrepreneurship Bootcamp for Veterans with Disabilities.

Changing the World One Business at a Time

When companies seek to deepen their positive impact, they win. When they lose sight of their ideals, they fail. That was the experience of AOL's vice chairman, Ted Leonsis. AOL's original company mission was "to build a global medium as central to people's lives as the telephone and television—and even more valuable." During the years that the company stayed true to that vision, it grew. But the day came when it merged with Time Warner, and its "higher calling" changed— the prime objective was no longer to improve the lives of others. The focus and intention shifted. AOL had to "deliver $11 billion in EBITDA (earnings before interest, taxes, depreciation, and amortization) to Wall Street." In other words, the new urgent priority was to line the investors' pockets on a demanding payback schedule. That was the same day that user numbers and the brand began their decline. The product and service didn't change, but the company's intention did, and it changed everything. Before, Leonsis had been happily challenged by the ideal: to empower people with connectivity and transform the culture. With the focus now on benefiting the few rather than the many, the company floundered. Users were increasingly disgruntled, and profits eventually collapsed.

Leonsis sums up the lesson this way: "When the company and its employees, partners, and users were happy, AOL flourished. When these constituencies were unhappy, it spiraled down. It was a simple formula. Make multiple communities happy and all will be well. Fail to do so, and it all falls apart."

Where Do I Start?

Where do you start when you're the little guy? The same place as when you're a corporate CEO or a billionaire: right where you are. Start by doing something about what incites you or excites you. The seasoned entrepreneur always sees needs as opportunities.

The new entrepreneurs seek to remedy inequity. It's our nature to want to do better. As an entrepreneur, you are already being of service. Find those areas where it doesn't take much to have an impact. Start there. Get into creative problem-solving mode. Brainstorm ways you can expand your current business model, resources, product, service, expertise, or time into other areas where you see a need that appeals to you.

The following ideas on how to grow your ability to affect others apply to for-profits and nonprofits, CEOs and start-ups, at work and at home. Use them to get inspired, and write down every idea you get as you read through these last chapters. To contribute is an absolute entrepreneurial essential.

1. Have a Small Impact Every Day

I was with a group of philanthropists on a trip to South Africa, where we visited a Cape Town orphanage, bringing supplies and donations. In 2001, when the HIV/AIDS pandemic had left thousands of children without parents, a local woman with a day-care center opened her doors to house as many orphans as she could, including several babies who had been left by the roadside. The moment

I walked in, a young boy about five years old came running across the room toward me with his arms wide open and a big smile on his face. As he reached out to me, I swept him up in my arms and held him in a big hug. We were complete strangers who didn't even speak the same language, yet we certainly had a connection. In that moment, it hit me: it doesn't take much to have an impact. And the impact seemed mutual. The rest of the day, this boy wouldn't let go of me.

I learned later that he had been picked up six months earlier off the streets where he had been left to die. I thought, "And I complain when someone puts mayonnaise on my sandwich? This kid has known more hardship than most adults, yet he can still open up to love."

Someone took a picture of me reaching down to this little boy who was reaching up to me, both of us smiling like long-lost brothers. I keep the photo on my cell phone. It reminds me, we don't need words or money to make a connection—the connection itself makes the difference.

When we follow our best instincts, the heart opens wide. Only then is it obvious how much we can do for each other. That little boy gave me a glimpse into what I have to give. I pull out that photo sometimes to remind myself that

I can live every day on purpose—to feel fulfilled. In each moment, I can choose how I want to influence others.

I hope this book helps you to see how much you have to give. We can't really know what is inside us until we give it away.

2. Lose Yourself in Something that Warms Your Heart

Since Nido Qubein came on as president of High Point University, it has risen to *U.S. News & World Report's* number one ranking among up-and-coming colleges. When asked how he grew the brand so quickly and continues to find the funding to expand beyond all expectations, Qubein insists that the school is *everyone's* success, because those who contribute to fulfilling its potential also benefit from it. He attributes the success to what he calls "intentional congruence": the faculty, support staff, students, trustees, alumni, and even the city residents and government officials all share the same focus and intention. "The miracle is in the mix," Qubein explains. "Our beliefs direct our results . . . Our faith strengthens our actions. We focus on possibility thinking, not on restrictive analysis. We believe that out of adversity can emerge abundance . . . Here we focus on our students, not on the product (the diploma) but the product of the product: what will they do with their lives? How will they change the world? Who will they influence? Where will they construct a positive career?"

3. Use Capitalism for a Cause

Milton Hershey had a lot of heart. Though he grew up quite poor and failed at his first few business ventures, he never let go of his progressive ideals and utopian vision. In fact, he used his idealism, as Walt Disney did, to build a lasting legacy that still thrives today.

After he opened his chocolate factory on Pennsylvania farmland, developing the community became a lifelong passion for him. Hershey gave an entire community jobs and newly built homes, then built an amusement park that soon became another source of local prosperity. At one point, he even tried to turn his profitable and growing department store into a co-op for the entire community. He believed that "co-operation is the basis of the ideal state of the future." Unfortunately, the townspeople, who could not stretch their minds around the idea, turned him down. In 1909, Hershey opened a small orphanage for boys, which eventually became the Milton Hershey School and has provided homes and education to thousands of children in need of a safe, supportive environment for their primary through high school years. And later, during the Second World War, he supplied over three billion chocolate Ration D bars and Tropical bars to U.S. military personnel all over the world.

At some point, a company has to move from being entrepreneur-centric to vision-centric. Far more benefits arise when purpose, rather than profit, drives the enterprise.

To be honest, when I first opened the karate studio, I was thinking, *this is a great idea because I can work out regularly while bringing in a second income.* At first, I didn't see all the potential we had to make a real difference in so many lives. Once upon a time, I was an autocratic and overbearing employer. And I thought this was leadership . . . until the day I found out that most of my staff hated working for me. That was a real eye-opener—and an opportunity. I realized that the least effective way of getting anyone to do anything was by demanding it. So when I opened the studio, I tried new ways of "doing leadership." I wanted my employees to feel they were a part of something meaningful, and as I tried to let them experience their own leadership, we became a much more cohesive team. At no time was this cohesiveness more evident than when I returned to the studio for the first time after my accident.

I had been away, rehabbing at home, for months and was getting increasingly worried about what was happening at the school. I remember the first day I walked in—very slowly because I was in pain and still in a neck brace. All the teachers and students turned to me. I was thinner and still having trouble speaking, so I stuttered a little. I said, "I was thinking of not coming back until after I was all healed, so you would never see or hear me like this and it would be as if I had never had an accident. And then I thought, I could do that or I could allow you to be part of my fight back to health, so that we share my moments of struggle and my moments of triumph—and there will be many. You kids are the reason I put the helmet on that day that probably saved my life. So you're entitled to be part of my fight back."

It was an amazing experience for me. I watched my students and staff demonstrate their willingness to step up in the face of my vulnerability. They told me hopeful stories of others they knew who had gotten through hardship. They opened doors for me, literally. I couldn't even get past the door without getting half a dozen hugs. And they worked harder at demonstrating mastery in their practice, to show me they were working hard. They impressed me. I think they learned more about leadership when I was vulnerable than when I was strong. And so did I.

4. Set Higher Standards for Yourself

There have always been certain people who seem to live their life outside society's acceptable standards. Rather than slip below the standard for what is acceptable, they transcend it altogether. They set far higher standards for themselves than anyone else would ever require. In their personal pursuit of an ideal, they raise the bar for everyone. Patagonian CEO Yvon Chouinard is one of those. While intensely self-directed, he is also extremely aware of his greater earthly environment. By going far outside mere self-concern, he has concerned his business with all living things.

Patagonia went to great lengths and great expense to create new fabrics and figure out painstaking new processes for milling organic cotton. Other companies were able to replicate his new system, which cut back on chemical processing. But that still wasn't far enough as far as Yvon Chouinard was concerned. And he *was* concerned. He was concerned about the environment and our continued existence in it. As soon as he recognized that the mass production of organic cotton still had its own set of detrimental effects, he took the experiment further. He strove to cut out the use of petroleum products. This resulted in the invention of an entirely new type of manufactured fabric: a neoprene that uses merino wool and recycled polyester.

To date, Patagonia has given at least $46 million to grassroots environmentally conscious organizations. By his unwavering commitment to his ideals, it's very possible that he has begun a revolution in business on several fronts. At least five hundred separate organizations and businesses have signed on to Chouinard's initiative called "One Percent for the Planet." They have agreed to donate 1 percent of their gross revenues to environmental causes.

5. Have a Vision and Get on a Mission

One of the best ways to ensure that you contribute to the world around you is to craft your company's mission carefully, based on your core values—the ideals you have arrived at on your Vision Wall. Start by studying the mission and visions of the companies you love and want to emulate. Missions can change over time, and that informs everyone of their new priorities and plans. Here is the progression of Facebook's mission statements over the years:

- ". . . connects people through social networks at colleges."
- ". . . helps you connect and share with the people in your life."
- ". . . gives people the power to share and make the world more open and connected."

The evolution of Mark Zuckerberg's thinking grew from a mile radius around him on the Harvard campus to the world at large. When your values and your vision grow, so does your business and your impact.

Remember AOL's original mission statement? "To build a global medium as central to people's lives as the telephone or television, and even more valuable." That's a bold claim, and the company achieved exactly that within a few years, by 2000. That was when Wall Street's mandate superseded the company's own. When you study the rise and fall of great companies, it becomes obvious how the mindset is the engine behind the marketing, mechanics, and ultimately the money side of business deals. AOL didn't arrive at a new mission for another six years, during which it floundered without that clarity of purpose. By serving a new master, the company lost sight of its vision and, perhaps, its values. All the platforms it had initiated were instead made popular by MySpace and Facebook. Now AOL's mission is "to serve the world's most engaged community"—ambiguous at best, and probably not enough to rally the troops and gain momentum again in the new marketplace.

What is your calling? Think of your business as your contribution. This is not only the most exciting and rewarding standpoint from which to grow a business, it is also the most effective. When you are compelled to make a difference in your world, however big or small, you are willing to reach far beyond what you know, toward what you and your creation—your company—can become. You are pulled forward by a higher mandate than money and accolades.

To access free training and more resources go to:
www.theentrepreneurssolution.com/resources

CHAPTER 20

GROWTH: BE A CATALYST FOR CHANGE

What goes into the chemistry of change: moment meets messenger, information becomes action. Hearts and minds shift to a new paradigm, money happens, and it all comes together.
—**Nancy Brinker**

CONTRIBUTION = Purpose + Growth

Watching an Oakland Raiders game with Jeremy the other day, I kept noticing flashes of pink during every tackle and pass. "When did the Raiders change their team color to pink?" I asked. Then, taking a closer look at the TV, I saw that the opposing team was wearing pink cleats and helmets, too. That's when I realized that it was a show of support for Susan G. Komen for the Cure, Nancy Brinker's Breast Cancer foundation. And what better way to bring national attention to the cause than by dressing football players in pink for the whole month of October. I thought, wow, how many high-level TV and NFL execs, agents, and managers had to sign off on an investment in pink cleats? Thirty years ago, no one even wanted to utter the word "breast" or "cancer" except behind closed doors. Now we are asked at the supermarket checkout line if we want to add a dollar to our purchase to support the foundation. FritoLay packages its healthy chips in pink bags. A sea of women in pink runs through the streets of fifty-seven U.S. cities and countless other countries to "Race for the Cure," sponsored by Samsung and other major corporations. Years of clever marketing and creative collaborations, with the tireless help of thousands of volunteers, have made that pink ribbon ubiquitous.

How did a mom from Peoria, Illinois, struggling to deal with the devastating loss of her sister, come to affect the global community on so many levels?

The achievement came directly from Nancy Brinker's commitment to fulfill a promise she made to her sister: to end the silence around this disease and make life better for families touched by it. With no entrepreneurial experience, she initially doubted her abilities, but it was the clarity of her goal, the courage she got from her sister, Susan G. Komen, and her tenacious character that made her persist. As a loving, committed sister *(identity)*, she was driven by her sense of justice *(ideal)* to find the cure *(intention)*. Guided by her husband's wisdom as a CEO, she developed a uniquely entrepreneurial model to fund her cause and make it *everyone's* cause. From her marketing background, she understood that perception was key but people were everything. So in the beginning, she presented her fledgling foundation as bigger than it really was. This gave her influence, which she then used to make an impact. She had a talent for connecting with anyone and everyone she met, then putting a bug in their ear about how they could contribute to something important. She gave them a chance to be part of something greater than their own cares and concerns, and she always made it fun. Though it is a terribly sad and serious topic, she created an atmosphere of community and celebration. Then, at some point, her little start-up was an international phenomenon.

The results included $1.5 billion toward new technologies and research to discover breast cancer's cause and cure, increased worldwide awareness and preventive education, first-of-their-kind programs for women in developing countries, better support for families, and a global community of people who support each other in their shared wish to cure this disease that has touched us all in some way. How was all this possible? In Brinker's own words, "What goes into the chemistry of change: moment meets messenger, information becomes action. Hearts and minds shift to a new paradigm, money happens, and it all comes together."

Fulfill Your Promise and Potential

Success and fulfillment are not the same. Success comes from completing your goals, ticking off a checklist of criteria that marks your progress in getting what you want. And that is always gratifying—to a point. Fulfillment comes from going beyond your own wants to get others what *they* need, which is rewarding. The new entrepreneur sees social needs as opportunities and looks to gain the greatest rewards for everyone on all sides of the equation.

If the voice inside you right now is insisting, "But I'm just an entrepreneur; I can't go out there and change the world," then you aren't really getting what it means to be an entrepreneur. You can start your business because you need money to get by. Or you can develop a company to fulfill a greater promise to yourself and everyone else it touches. You can say, "Well, I don't have to take care of other people's problems. It's up to them to take care of it." Or you can say, as Branson does, "I will to do something because I *can*." Running the operation is going to be a lot of work whether you do it for yourself or for something greater. So wouldn't you rather create much bigger opportunities to expand in surprising, amazing ways?

It's interesting to note that corporate success is measured by profits, while a social entrepreneur's success is usually measured by the impact on a community or country in need (for example, changes in government policy and practice, or increase in a village's economic activity). But even those differences are lessening as social enterprises gain more access to financial resources, and corporations gain more access to markets through social enterprises. TOMS Shoes is a great example of a model that achieves both measures of success: profit and positive change.

1. Stay True to What Matters to You

TOMS Shoes founder and Chief Shoe Giver Blake Mycoskie's sense of responsibility for the environment forced him to get creative about how his company manufactured shoes, how it accomplished product fulfillment and delivery, and even how it put its office together: with recycled materials and natural ventilation so it never has to burn energy unnecessarily with air-conditioning or heating. The demonstration of his commitment has also inspired other companies to rethink the way they do business.

As his company improves the quality of life for millions around the world, Mycoskie finds that it also improves his own:

The greatest thing that has happened in my life since starting TOMS is that I've learned that you need very little to be happy. And I've learned from the people that I've given shoes to . . . they've given more to me than I have to them. When you give someone something like a pair of shoes, you're saying, "You matter." That message is as important as the shoes.

2. Use Your Gifts and Follow Your Own Mandate

Oprah Winfrey has the gift of empathy, coupled with the gift of gab. Her grandmother saw it in her when Oprah, at three years old, started interviewing her dolls. When Oprah's early career as a news reporter required her to be objective, she was unhappy, stressed out, and nearly fired from her job. When she shifted into being a talk show host, her natural personality thrived and won over millions of viewers. Yet, something kept tugging at her to move beyond what was working for her—sensationalized tabloid topics—toward topics closer to her heart: family hardships, spirituality, charity work, women's issues, and world politics to name a few. Now she is considered one of the hundred most influential people of the twenty-first century, and the most philanthropic celebrity in history. This is what happens when we get to the heart of what our mission really is, and allow it to lead us.

She conveys her singular message of compassion, community, and spiritual connection *(identity)* through every possible media outlet there is *(influence)*: her show, magazine, TV channel Oxygen, books, satellite radio, website and social media, and film, to uplift as many spirits as she can *(impact)*. And now she is launching the Oprah Winfrey Network (OWN TV): "devoted to self-discovery, to connecting you to your best self and to the world." It's pretty easy to see what matters to her. Oprah is led to fulfill a greater responsibility in the world: to inspire us all to reach for our greatest potential. It's no coincidence, then, that in 2010, Oprah, alongside Jesus Christ, Galileo, and Einstein, made it onto *Life* magazine's list of the top one hundred people who changed the world.

3. Stay Aligned With Your Core Values

What you find rewarding may change along the way. Listen to what's really calling out to you. Remember your first entrepreneurial essential: clarity, which includes your core values, your unchanging *ideals*. Be clear from the start about what's important to you. In the beginning, when you are doing everything you can to get your business to take off, it's easy to think, "I just have to do this; then I will pay attention to my health/family/partner." Later, when business is good, it will be tempting to say, "I've got to keep this thing in the air. I'll have time for my health/family/partner later." Don't live on the Deferred Rewards Program.

A bigger vision produces bigger results. Be willing to play a larger role in your world, and stay attuned to your shifting priorities.

Bill Gates's initial mission was to put a computer in every living room in America. When Microsoft achieved something close to that, he expanded his vision into Africa. His new mandate? Eradicate polio, improve education, and reduce hunger and poverty in the world. Since leaving his day job at the Microsoft office to head up the Bill and Melinda Gates Foundation, he has come very close achieving his first objective. Polio cases in India and Nigeria have dropped 95 percent. Championing his favorite causes is now his labor of love.

Entrepreneurs love to set high goals, then see the visible results of their efforts. Progress energizes the vision and deepens their commitment. The entrepreneurial mind says, *well, if we can do that, what else is possible?* And now, instead of waiting to donate to charities at the end of their lives, the new entrepreneurs apply capitalist solutions to social causes. That is because they see the integral connection between a thriving people and a thriving economy.

4. Be Willing to Play a Greater Role

Sometimes you don't choose a cause. Rather, as in Nancy Brinker's case, it chooses you. You may be reluctant to pay attention at first. If it keeps tugging at your heartstrings, it's there for a good reason. Be willing to step forward, even before you know what the job will entail. The world is full of reluctant heroes. The ones we have actually heard of, whom we admire, are the ones who stepped up.

Have you ever had that experience of feeling inconvenienced because events beyond your control changed your plans, only later to realize that things worked out much better than you had planned?

Some gifted people don't have the dedication or desire to give their gift significance in the world. When you surrender to living your potential without a predetermined outcome, you take the walls down. The sky opens up. Boom! Your life expands beyond what you thought you were capable of. You don't ask, "Why me?" You wonder, "Well, then, if me, how can I use my gifts to lead and serve?"

It's called servant leadership. Most people totally misunderstand what it means to be of service. Service isn't a burden. It's a privilege.

Even if you feel unprepared for the task, you may still be seen as an example to others, a mentor or a teacher. Most great leaders throughout history doubted themselves along the way. And the fact is, if you are anything more than self-serving, you are already a leader. If you have a child or a family, you're a leader. Own a company? You're a leader. Do community service or random acts of kindness on any given day? You're a leader. Servant leadership is an honor and an opportunity.

5. Challenge Yourself

A sixteen-year-old girl named Abby Sunderland, from the town next to mine, set out to sail around the world alone last year. At thirteen, she had set a clear goal: to become the youngest sailor in history to circle the globe nonstop. When her seventeen-year-old brother attempted it and succeeded, she saw that it was actually possible

Abby said, "I had begun to think that dreams are meant to be no more than dreams and that in reality, dreams don't come true. Then my brother, Zac, left on his trip. It was amazing to see all the support that he got from around the world and to see how everyone worked together to help make his dream reality. Watching him do this really made me believe that I could, too."

After becoming the youngest person to sail around Cape Horn alone, she hit rough weather and thirty-foot swells just beyond Cape Town, South Africa. Four months into her adventure, and more than halfway to her goal, all communication was lost. Four days later, Sunderland was rescued and brought home. Though she didn't complete her mission, her greatest accomplishment was having made the decision to go for it. I hope she considered it a success—and a rewarding one— just for the fact that she rose to the challenge.

Challenge yourself to pursue your potential and watch the phenomenal results happen around you. Be an example for others. Be unreasonable. Try and fail. Then remember that it was a success, because you learned and grew in the process.

Desperately Seeking Entrepreneurs

The greatest challenge right now is for entrepreneurs to innovate new ways to bridge the gap between private business objectives and public needs. More than ever, MBA grads are choosing to bring their gifts and knowledge to bear in social organizations rather than in corporate jobs. New models are arising out of the pioneering work of Yale graduate Bill Drayton's Ashoka Foundation, which funds the best and brightest social entrepreneurs in the world. In fact, he coined the phrase "social entrepreneurship" in 1980, when he became an "innovator for the public." The Ashoka Foundation's mission is to "shape a global, entrepreneurial, competitive citizen sector: one that allows social entrepreneurs to thrive and enables the world's citizens to think and act as changemakers."

Procter and Gamble gets it. The company has created a new division called P&G Futureworks to connect and develop innovative entrepreneurs. Its corporate objective is to extend its reach into new regions. Toward that end, the company provides financial support, experienced people, and in-kind services to its entrepreneurial venture, Healthpoint Services. Together they provide access to safe drinking water, healthcare services, and medicines for rural communities in India. The collaboration helps both the profit and nonprofit reach their social and financial goals. This is just one model that bridges the functional gap between serving private and public interests.

The burgeoning model is called a *hybrid value chain*. It works well for everyone involved because companies tap into new markets, and social enterprises increase their reach in the community to provide more resources. With more access to resources, low-income populations improve their quality of life, and this, in turn, often generates jobs and creates new emerging economies. This is a sustainable win-win-win that supports corporation, cause, and community by finding the intersection where their needs and objectives meet and complement each other. It's an entrepreneurial solution that fuses philanthropic, public, and profit sectors, making all sides indispensible to one another.

When the Future Calls, Answer

As if that partnership were not exciting enough, P&G Futureworks wants to help *you* grow to help it grow. It is actively seeking "fledgling businesses currently serving new market businesses." Its mission is to become an "entrepreneurial new-business generator, transforming those fledgling businesses that can scale to serve the mass market . . . If you currently are running such a business and believe P&G can help you grow fast, then FutureWorks wants to hear from you!"

> To access free training and more resources go to:
> **www.theentrepreneurssolution.com/resources**

CHAPTER 21

AND YOUR JOURNEY
CONTINUES . . .

Sometimes it's the journey that teaches you a lot about your destination
—Drake

N
ow that you have been introduced to and better understand all the Nine Entrepreneurial Essentials, let's look at how they fit together and how the mind-set quadrant model works. Just like me, I am sure that as you read through the Nine Entrepreneurial Essentials (Clarity, Courage, Character, Connect, Collaborate, Capitalize, Commit, Create and Contribute), you reflect on what level of activation do you have for each of these essentials? If not, you should be consistently evaluating your position, activity and outcomes just the same as the pilot checks their instruments to determine that they are still on track.

NINE ENTREPRENEURIAL ESSENTIALS ™

What do you stand for?

Clarity   Commit

How are you going to show up?

Courage

Create

Character

Contribute

Connect

Capitalize

Collaborate

Are you living your calling?

This will provide you insights into the areas that need to be focused on from a mind-set perspective. Mind-set is not a destination, it is an ever-expansive journey that you will constantly be on. It will ultimately permeate everything you do in life, it will help you decide what you will do, how you will do it, with whom you will do it with and the persistence that you will apply to it. You will find that mind-set really isn't just about business and being entrepreneur but about life in general and how you approach things including relationship and even parenting. In order to assist you in evaluating your level, we have developed a quadrant process model as you see below that allows you through answering the various assessment questions to place yourself within the quadrant. This then will allow you to determine the areas that may need additional focus.

The X and Y-axes of the model create the four quadrants. The X-axis represents your mind-set, and the Y-axis represents your success sustainability. Each quadrant is labeled based on the characteristics that typically prevail at that level. For instance, a Task Mechanic is typically a "worker bee" who stays on automatic pilot, running on the same treadmill every day based on the tasks they receive from their managers or even from life itself. They are simply doing as they are told, with scant regard for their own fulfillment, dreams, ideals, or desires. One of the challenges at this level is how people see their *identity.* This is why the prescriptive transition at this level involves the elements that we discussed in Part

1 of the book, on refining and further developing one's identity. Additionally, the Task Mechanic will need to work through the elements in Part 3 of the book to move into the higher quadrants.

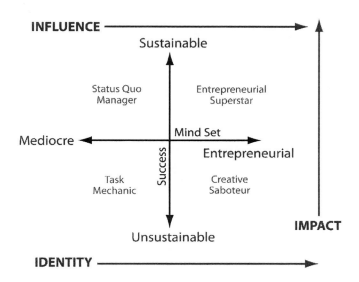

The person in the lower-right quadrant, the Creative Saboteur, is typically someone who is a regular idea machine. These people are tremendously creative, constantly coming up with all sorts of entrepreneurial ideas. But they lack consistent and focused execution. Thus, they don't stick with any idea long enough to bring it fruition. In this quadrant, the prescriptive transition entails developing more *impact* with your business and ideas, through the elements discussed in Part 3 of the book.

The upper-left quadrant represents the Status Quo Manager, who is focused simply on keeping things from falling apart—keeping things moving along as they have in the past. This is a sustainable but not very expansive mind-set. Status Quo Managers need to focus on the elements of *influence*, *from* Part 2 of this book. By doing so, they will further develop the skills and mind-set of entrepreneurship through better understanding how to influence themselves, internally, as well as the external elements of their entrepreneurial world. Ultimately, you want to be consistently operating in the upper-right quadrant—that of the Entrepreneurial Superstar. This is where your mind-set is at its most productive, and sustainable success is at its highest.

The key to understanding and implementing this model is to think of it as your own personal entrepreneurial mind-set locator. It's like having the map app on the iPhone—by using the iPhone/iPad App assessment tool on our website, you can place yourself on the quadrant model. Also, keep in mind that where you are in the quadrant model will shift from time to time and over time.

Statistics show that half of businesses fail within the first few years, 80 percent within the first five years, and as much as 96 percent by year ten. This is not necessarily because they were bad businesses (although some certainly were). Many of the failures were a result of not having the first element of the Business Mastery Blueprint™ right. All the other elements—*marketing, mechanics,* and *money*—depend on *mind-set*. By now you see how the mind-set permeates and affects every aspect of business. Gaining the clarity, vision, culture, philosophy, and congruency will automatically push your business to the head of the pack. Most business owners don't do the necessary detail work, as you have done here, to gain an in-depth understanding of their business.

Imagine yourself for a moment, fifteen years from now, looking back on the path you created and the lives you touched along the way. Imagine what it will feel like to know how many families you have fed through the years, how many causes you have benefited, and all the lives that are forever changed because you stepped up and made the decision to live by *The Entrepreneur's Solution.* The interesting thing is to realize that you have changed not only the lives of your employees and team members but of every generation that follows. Because you chose to pick up this book and read it all the way through. Because you decided to buck the tide of naysayers and critics and *do it.* Because you chose to live the life of your choosing, outside the model of mediocrity, and thereby created an example for all to follow—and follow they will. You are now part of the entrepreneur class.

You now know inside yourself how to create the strongest and longest-lasting foundation for your business by applying the elements of *The*

Entrepreneur's Solution via your *identity, influence,* and *impact.* This is the beginning of your journey toward a great legacy that, until now, you could only imagine. By applying what you know now, you are set to realize it. You have gained a clarity that wasn't there before, through nurturing your innate ability to focus, to hold your vision constantly in front of you in an emotionally compelling way.

You have prepared your mind to produce the best results, just as a farmer prepares the soil by tilling and tending it and fertilizing it with all the needed nutrients so the crops will flourish and thrive. In your case, it is your mind-set, philosophy, and perspective that have been nurtured, tended, and cultivated through the building blocks of *influence*—the ability to *connect, collaborate,* and *capitalize*—to create a synergistic environment where all your ideas, products, and services will flourish. Then, by harvesting these through the larger arena of *impact*—by *committing, creating, and contributing*—you will create a business built on higher *ideals, intentions,* and *purpose,* resulting in a legacy that will surpass your wildest expectations. It will do so because you have learned how to serve a higher purpose than just the bottom line.

So where to from here? It is time to take your harvest to market! To ensure a prosperous crop every year, continue to till the soil by applying these Nine Entrepreneurial Essentials in your business, at every stage of your growth (I have provided a 3X3 matrix of all the essential building blocks to use as a quick reference This is not just a starter kit to get you off the ground. *The Entrepreneur's Solution* gives you the timely resources you need to support and sustain your company through whatever challenges arise. It is also timeless in that it has the power to expand your success beyond what you may now believe is possible—as long as you execute. A blueprint is the plan for building your future.

Remember, mastery is one of the keys and building blocks of *The Entrepreneur's Solution.* So reach out for continued growth opportunities. You may want to consider attending one of our Business Breakthrough Academy workshops to dive deeper into *The Entrepreneur's Solution* and the Business Mastery Blueprint™. Seek out your mentors, those who have already achieved something close to what you want to accomplish. Whether it's me or someone else, make sure your mentors know how to take your game to a higher level and raise your standards toward the unreasonable. I say "unreasonable" because those who live in the realm of the unreasonable will be the ones who also live in the world of possibility. They will represent our bigger, brighter, and better future. They are you. The future is in your hands now. Take it and embrace it. Change the future and our culture for the better. You are the change the world needs to see. Give it what it is hungry for. And remember, what you do matters!

Until we meet again, welcome to your journey. Make your journey epic, your vision grand, and legacy significant!

The Entrepreneur's Solution Matrix

THE ENTREPRENEUR'S SOLUTION

STAGES		COMMIT = CONSISTENCY + MASTERY	CREATE = VERSATILITY + FLEXIBILITY	CONTRIBUTE = GROWTH + PURPOSE	IMPACT	TRANSITION
	REALIZATION					
	MOTIVATION	CONNECT = COMMUNICATION + EMPATHY	COLLABORATE = INNOVATION + PARTNERING	CAPITALIZE = MONETIZATION + PERCEPTION	INFLUENCE	
	ACTIVATION	CLARITY = VISION + FOCUS	COURAGE = RESPONSIBILITY + CONFIDENCE	CHARACTER = ACTION + CONVICTION	IDENTITY	

To access free training and more resources go to:
www.theentrepreneurssolution.com/resources

ABOUT THE AUTHOR

Mel is the founder of Business Breakthrough Academy and Thoughtpreneur Academy where he helps entrepreneurs bring their businesses to the world and build the lifestyle that they want. Mel is one the most sought after entrepreneurial mentor and strategic thinkers of our time. Unlike many other so called "business coaches," Mel has lived everything he teaches and continues to do so. Mel has built, bought and sold numerous multimillion-dollar businesses for himself as well as his clients. Mel's strategies have helped build thousands of businesses and have generated hundreds of millions of dollars for his clients, ranging from large corporations to startups and small family-owned businesses.

Mel is a true believer in the entrepreneurial way of life and says that this "new frontier" is the paradigm that will shift society from simply existing to living life bigger, bolder and on their own terms.

Mel helps business owners and entrepreneurs build meaningful businesses so that they can have more profit, fans and freedom. His principles help customers become raving fans and your life full with fulfillment from a business that is congruent with your values, in alignment with your higher vision and connected to all stakeholders at an emotional level.

Mel is a committed advocate for the entrepreneurial way and provides real education, to real entrepreneurs for creating a real life! After all, we are placed here to create a legacy beyond acquiring, achieving and accomplishing but by connecting at a meaningful level and impacting lives through our businesses, services and ideals each and every day.

Some of Mel's career highlights include:

- Globally recognized thought leader, business advisor, CPA and financial expert.
- Created and implemented growth strategies including taking a company from $50 million to over $200 million.
- Assisted in numerous high-stakes negotiations, settlements and transactions.
- Has advised entrepreneurs from startups to multi-million dollar and billion dollar companies as to what drives value and how to build their dreams.
- Creator of multiple entrepreneurial training programs that provide the keys to business growth and success based on road-tested and proven processes and systems.
- Authored and co-authored numerous texts, articles and programs that has reached thousands around the country.

Find more resources, training and subscribe to Mel's blog at:
Website: www.MelAbraham.com
Facebook: https://www.facebook.com/melhabraham
Blog: http://melabraham.tumblr.com/
YouTube: https://www.youtube.com/user/MelHAbraham
LinkedIn: http://www.linkedin.com/in/melhabraham

CPSIA information can be obtained at www.ICGtesting.com
Printed in the USA
LVOW12s0522100415

434033LV00003BB/115/P